MW01056675

DESTINATION
UNKNOWN

ESSENTIALS FOR CHRISTIAN Youth!

DESTINATION UNKNOWN

50 QUICK MYSTERY TRIPS FOR YOUTH GROUPS

BY SAM HALVERSON

DESTINATION UNKNOWN
50 QUICK MYSTERY TRIPS FOR YOUTH GROUPS

Copyright © 2001 by Abingdon Press.

All rights reserved.
With the exception of those items so noted, no part of this work may be reproduced or transmitted in any form or by any means, electronic or mechanical, including photocopying and recording, or by any information storage or retrieval system, except as may be expressly permitted by the 1976 Copyright Act or in writing from the publisher. Requests for permission should be addressed to Abingdon Press, 201 Eighth Avenue South, Nashville, TN 37202.

This book is printed on acid-free, recycled paper.

ISBN 0-687-09724-X

Scripture quotations marked (CEV) are from the Contemporary English Version Copyright ©1991, 1992, 1995 by American Bible Society. Used by permission.

Scripture quotations marked (*Message*) are taken from *THE MESSAGE*. Copyright © Eugene H. Peterson, 1993, 1994, 1995. Used by permission of NavPress Publishing Group.

Scripture quotations marked (NIV) are taken from HOLY BIBLE, NEW INTERNATIONAL VERSION®. NIV®. Copyright © 1973, 1978, 1984 by International Bible Society. Used by permission of Zondervan Publishing House. All rights reserved.

Scripture quotations marked (NRSV) are taken from the *New Revised Standard Version of the Bible*, copyright 1989, Division of Christian Education of the National Council of Churches of Christ in the United States of America. Used by permission. All rights reserved.

01 02 03 04 05 06 07 08 09 10—10 9 8 7 6 5 4 3 2 1

TABLE OF Contents - - -

FROM THE Author

When I first began planning an event called, "Destination Unknown" for my youth group the youth quickly renamed it "Destination Unthought-Of." As much as they liked the intrigue and mystery around the event, some believed that I chose not to tell them where we were going so that I would not have to think about it until we left the parking lot. Looking back, I realize that their perception may have originated from my response to their question of "Where are we going?" with "I'm making this up as I go along."

> Years later when your youth pass by that ruined house or those three crosses, they will be likely to recall the Scripture lesson they learned there.

The programs in this book will involve a bit more planning than "making it up as you go along." Though the book is called *Destination Unknown*, it is not essential that the locations be kept secret from the youth group. The mystery does help, though, as the youth begin to wonder and talk about where they will go next. I found it more interesting to say, "We're going to a secret destination tonight that will help you understand John 10:1-18," than to say, "We're going to a sheepfold." Youth would ask, "What's in John 10?" and I'd respond, "Read it and find out. Then try to guess where we're going tonight."

The most important part about these programs is how they link the locations from around your community with Scripture and faith issues. Years later when your youth pass by that ruined house or those three crosses, they will be likely to recall the Scripture lesson they learned there.

While there is some planning involved, you will find things easy to put together. In fact, you may decide to hand a few programs over to some of the youth, allowing them to lead in the planning and discussion that follow (after all, the best way to learn is to plan and teach). As the youth see what you've planned and how you've connected the Scriptures with their own surroundings they will certainly recognize that you care for their faith development and that you're not simply "making it up as you go along."

—Sam Halverson

Before the Event

Prepare

Mystery makes these programs fun. However, parents do not usually like mystery when it comes to your taking their kids. They will want to know where you are going and what you'll be doing. Here are some ideas of how to prepare and inform the parents:

- Mail note cards a week in advance with your destination information and an RSVP to ensure that they've seen it and consent to the trip;
- Hold a parents' meeting about five minutes before you leave (when the parents are dropping off their youth) and inform them of your destination; and
- Recruit a volunteer in charge of informing parents when youth are dropped off, or designate a volunteer to be the contact whom parents may call before the event day. Remind the parents not to tell the youth where they're going.

Promote

Promote each "Destination Unknown" by telling the youth when and where to meet, and then giving them a little hint of where they're going. The Scripture is a good hint to use. In the bulletin the week before, you could say, *Next Sunday at 7 P.M. the youth group will go on a Destination Unknown. The location is a secret, but read John 6:33-51 for a clue.* Another great way to promote your "Destination Unknown" is to mail out cards with a map to the location and tell the youth what time to meet you there. If the youth meet you at the destination, spend a few minutes prior to the program to discuss the "On the Way" section.

Plan

Plan for more drivers than you expect. It's easier to tell a parent that they don't need to drive than to tell a youth that there is no room for him or her to come along. Do not allow youth to drive other youth to the destination from the church. If you have sent maps to have the youth meet you at the destination, you are not responsible. However, if you allow youth to drive other youth to the destination from the church, you are very responsible if anything should happen. Make sure your parents understand this rule so that they can support you.

Check with your church insurance agent to ensure that your youth are covered on these outings. Insurance on church-owned vehicles like vans or buses usually covers anyone riding in that vehicle. Be certain that your volunteer drivers also have coverage if they are using their own vehicles.

Although permission slips usually do not have any legal bearing, they are necessary for medical information and to ensure that you do have the parent's permission to take the youth to your destination. When a parent signs a permission slip, he or she is consciously recognizing that the church staff and volunteers are not responsible for injury or accident. The slip should also give permission for a doctor's care should such need arise. Make a slip that covers any trips you take for the full year, and you won't have to keep coming to your parents asking for another signature. You may photocopy the slip provided on page 8.

Using *Destination Unknown* With Small Groups

The best way to use these programs is with small groups; leading fewer youth in these programs will have a much greater impact.

As you plan a "Destination Unknown" for your youth group meetings, consider Jesus' words, "Where two or three are gathered in my name, I am there among them" (Matthew 18:20).

Smaller groups allow for a level of intimacy in discussion that cannot happen in larger groups. If your group is less than ten, great! You're already a small group.

If you have a large youth group, consider breaking into smaller groups. If you have a small group ministry, send different groups with their leaders. Try sending Sunday school classes or separating the youth by age levels, interests, or gender.

YOUTH PROGRAM PERMISSION SLIP
For June 1, 20__ through May 31, 20__
Please return this completed form to the church office.

Youth Name:_____

Grade:_____   Age:_____

Address:_____

_____

E-mail:_____

Phone:_____   School:_____

School address:_____

School phone:_____

Allergies:_____

Other medical conditions:_____

_____

Parent(s) or guardian(s) name(s):_____

Home phone:_____ Work phone:_____

Cell phone:_____ Pager:_____

E-mail:_____

Please provide names of persons to contact if parent(s) or guardian(s) cannot be reached.

1. Name:_____ Home phone:_____
   Work phone:_____ Cell phone:_____
2. Name:_____ Home phone:_____
   Work phone:_____ Cell phone:_____
3. Name:_____ Home phone:_____
   Work phone:_____ Cell phone:_____

The above has my permission to participate on the _____*[church name here]*_____ Church youth ministry events between June 1, 20__ and May 31, 20__. I also understand that _____*[church name here]*_____ is not liable should injury come to my child. I give permission for emergency medical care to be given by a hospital should my child need such treatment before I am contacted.

Signature of parent or guardian:

_____

Insurance company and number: _____

Doctor's name:_____

Doctor's address:_____

Doctor's phone:_____

Permission is granted to photocopy this permission slip for groups using *Destination Unknown*. ©2001 Abingdon Press.

WHAT'S INSIDE

Scripture and Focus

Look at these sections together when planning your destinations. Use the Scripture index (page 143) to find a program that might touch on where you think God wants to take your group. Read the focus statement and destination to see how well the program may fit with your location, your resources, and your youth. If your church uses the *Revised Common Lectionary*, link Scriptures used in morning worship with the corresponding destination.

The Location

If possible, choose a site near where your youth live. That way your youth will be reminded of the lesson there whenever they pass by or visit there again. Find your sites early. You will find suggestions in each program for how to prepare for the "Destination Unknown." Double check with any necessary contacts the week before your group is scheduled to arrive. If the site you've chosen is outdoors, make alternate rain plans either by picking an alternate program from the book or making things fairly dry and comfortable at the site.

On the Way

This section of the program gives you ideas of how to prepare the youth for the program. You don't need to spend a lot of time on this. Just begin the discussion and let the youth take it from there. Don't feel like you have to direct the conversation. The point is to get the youth thinking about the issue or the upcoming experience before they even know what it is.

At the Site

Remember that you want the youth to link the site with the Scripture and what they will learn. Look at the focus statement once more before beginning the program. Try to keep things centered on that statement. You may discover a teachable moment that isn't listed in the program but fits well with your kids' experience. Go with it.

Look through the main outline for the program and see if any activities or discussion questions may be led by some youth in your group. Allowing youth a chance to lead and direct the program brings them into the vision and mission of your ministry. Some of the discussion questions might be best handled in pairs or small groups, and these smaller groups can also be led by some older youth or by youth who have leadership potential.

Bright Ideas

You'll see suggestions marked "Bright Ideas." These will give you some creative and optional ways of using the program for other events or in other situations.

ACKNOWLEDGMENTS

Thanks to the youth groups of Northbrook United Methodist Church in Roswell, Georgia, Lovers Lane United Methodist Church in Dallas, Texas, Mount Bethel United Methodist Church in Marietta, Georgia, and First United Methodist Church in Lancaster, Ohio, for giving me the "testing ground" for these and other "Destination Unknowns." The adult volunteers in these and many churches continue to allow God's Holy Spirit to transform their ministry and their relationships into tools of discipleship and foundations of faith.

About the Author

Sam Halverson is an ordained minister of The United Methodist Church and works in the West Ohio Conference. He currently serves as a pastor at First United Methodist Church in Lancaster, Ohio where his wife, Kathy, and two children, Jesse and Megan, also attend. His ministry includes ministry with youth at the church as well as co-youth coordinator of the West Ohio Conference and serving on the Forum of Adults in Youth Ministry (FAYM) board. Sam leads workshops at national and local events for youth workers and is the author of *55 Group-Building Activities for Youth* and *Open Doors, Open Arms: How to Reach New Youth* (SkillAbilities Series).

DESTINATION

Focus: Youth will understand the strength of physical armor so that they can understand the strength of the "full armor of God."

Scripture: Ephesians 6:10–20

Location: A museum with historical suits of armor or a costume shop containing suits of armor

P aul uses the image of putting on the full armor of God in his letter to the Ephesians. Today that image is not quite so useful, since we rarely see someone decked out in a breastplate, shield, and helmet. Actually seeing and feeling the weight of the armor will help the youth understand the strength Paul tells us we have when we put on God's armor.

Though it may not be genuine, you may be able to find a suit of armor at a local antique mall or costume store. If possible, allow some of the youth to try it on.

Have markers and construction paper on hand for youth to make signs to tape on to the various parts of the armor: *truth, righteousness, proclaiming the gospel, faith, salvation,* and *Spirit.* In doing so, youth can see the full armor of God as a suit of armor. If you cannot try on the armor, have the youth tape the signs onto their clothes.

On the way:

Talk to the youth about what kinds of things make them feel safe and secure—physically, spiritually, mentally, and emotionally. The youth may mention things like their homes, their families, their friends, their faith, and their health.

At the site:

1. Talk a little about the different parts of the armor: what they were used for and what they are called. If it is possible to touch the armor, or to put on the suit, allow some time for the youth to touch it and wear it.

Notes

_____

_____

_____

_____

_____

_____

_____

_____

_____

_____

_____

_____

_____

_____

_____

2. Read the Scripture.

3. Have some paper ready for them to make signs of each part of the armor. Then have them tape their paper suits of armor to their clothes.

4. Discuss how each piece of the armor of God protects against evil. Continue your conversation from the car about what makes us feel safe. Then ask:
  - What makes us feel unsafe or in harm's way?

5. Ask:
  - What are some examples of evil in the world today?
  - Do you think it is possible to join the fight against evil?
  - What are some ways to fight evil?
  - How can the "armor of God" strengthen you and keep you safe in the battle against evil in the world?

6. Tell the youth that Paul was urging Christians not to fear evil but to work against it. Paul tells us that with the armor of God, we will overcome the battle with evil. Discuss battles they are facing right now.

7. Ask:
  - What part of the armor do you need most right now? Why?

8. Close with a prayer, asking God to seal the armor upon their souls and for the courage to join the battle.

9. Tell the youth to keep their signs and post them in their lockers or bedrooms so they will always remember that God is their shield and strength.

DESTINATION

Focus: Youth will direct their energy and strength on living for Christ as if they are preparing for a race or competition.

Scripture: 1 Corinthians 9:24-27

Location: A local or school athletic track

A school track or any local running track will help youth personalize Paul's image of "running to obtain the prize." As we encounter struggles in our faith, we can be sure that there is a prize when we reach the end of our race. Some tracks are used quite often through the week with practices and meets and people going through personal training. Check with whomever schedules the track (probably a school athletic director) so that you have an idea of when it is in use. If possible, use a track that will be seen regularly by youth in the future such as a school track or a track at a local fairgrounds. You could also add some fun by bringing along some string or ribbon to stretch across a finish line. If the coach or athletic director will give you access to the loudspeaker system, you could have a great time with someone "announcing" the race.

On the way:

Ask who in your group is actively involved in
sports. How much time does he or she spend each
week in training? Is all of his or her training with the rest of the team, or does he or she ever train independently? What does he or she do during the off season? What does he or she enjoy most—watching, training, or competing in sports? Why?

At the site:

1. As you walk on to the track, ask the youth to line up at a starting line. Tell them that they are going to run a short race. Set up a finish line at the fifty-meter mark. Allow some time for them to stretch or warm up and then ask them to run their best, assuring them that

Bright Idea!

If your local athletic track is so busy that you can't find a time when it is not in use, you could make some adaptations to this program and visit the track when there is a meet taking place. You would not be able to run a race during the meet, but you could run it in a parking lot or have the group watch a particular race in the meet instead.

there will be a prize at the end. When they are ready, yell out a countdown and a start signal. Be sure to furiously cheer them on.

2. After the race, invite the youth to sit on the ground inside the track or in the nearby stands. Pass out chocolate medals wrapped in gold to all the runners. (You can find these in most candy stores.) Celebrate that everyone finished the race and ran as hard as they could.

3. Read the Scripture. If possible, have it read over the loudspeaker.

4. Ask:
• What does a race have to do with our life with Christ?

Encourage the youth to draw some metaphors here: the goal of a race versus the goal of our life with Christ; how they deal with distractions in a race versus how they deal with distractions in their Christian race; the focus on the finish line versus our focus on only that which is of service to God; the focus on being first through the finish line versus helping others along the way; and the training before a race versus how we should prepare and train as Christians.

5. Ask:
• What does Paul mean when he says that runners "do it to get a crown that will not last; but we do it to get a crown that will last forever" (NIV, verse 25b)?

Point out that trophies and medals are just hunks of plastic or chocolate that will collect dust and not last forever. The prize we gain from God, though, is eternal and will never rust, break, nor tarnish.

Ask:
• What is the prize to which Paul is referring in these verses? (*eternal life with God*)

6. Talk for a few minutes about the race they just ran.

Ask:
• If this had been an Olympic race or an important meet, how would you have prepared?
• How do you prepare for your own race to receive God's prize?
• Is it easier to keep a training schedule for physical fitness or for spiritual fitness? Why?
• How would you train for spiritual fitness?
• What kinds of things stand in the way of such training?

14

7. Ask each individual to examine his or her level of spiritual training. Ask the youth to walk again to the track and to line up at the starting line. Tell them to look only at the finish line and to imagine where on the track ahead they would position themselves in their own spiritual race.

As they focus on that finish line, ask the following questions, pausing in between for the youth to quietly consider their answers:
- How well are you running your spiritual race?
- What kinds of things cause you to look around or away from the goal as you race?
- Who has been your "coach" as you prepare for your race?
- How can your coach help you more?
- Do you have other teammates who help you train for your spiritual race? Who are they? How can they encourage you in your training?

8. As a closing, ask the youth to walk as a group toward the finish line. As they walk, reread the Scripture loud enough for them to hear. Try to time it so that they cross the finish line when you read verse 27.

9. Encourage the youth to choose a mentor and peers—a "coach" and "teammates"—who will help them train for their spiritual races. If they already have some in mind, encourage them to talk with those persons and discuss ways they can be involved in the spiritual training of the youth.

10. Allow the youth a moment by themselves to walk around the track and talk with God about their positions in the race and where they need to be. When they are finished praying, gather them to leave.

Notes

DESTINATION

Bakery

Focus: Youth will watch the preparation of bread, connecting it as physical sustenance to spiritual sustenance that is Jesus Christ.

Scripture: John 6:33-51

Location: A bakery

Imagine the wonderful smell and warmth of a bakery as you and your group study what it means to feed on the bread of life, Jesus Christ. Those smells, tastes, and feelings will perhaps come back to your group when they smell bread, take Communion, or hear this Scripture in the future.

Find out when the bakery will be baking bread and try to go during that time. Ask if it would be possible for each person to try kneading and preparing a small loaf of bread. Bring along some grape juice and someone who is able to serve Communion.

On the way:

Ask the youth if they know the story from Exodus where God sent manna (bread from heaven) to the Hebrews in the wilderness so that they would have something to eat each day. If some know the story, ask them to tell it. If none do, then tell the story. Try to tell it in your own words rather than read it. The story is in Exodus 16. When the story has been told, explain that the group is going to a place where they will learn about a bread different from manna—the bread of life that, when eaten, gives eternal life.

At the site:

1. Ask the youth to listen and watch as the baker tells about making different breads. If possible, have the youth prepare small loaves for baking. Then wait as the bread bakes. (Be sure to prepare a kind of bread that doesn't take long to bake. If the bread is not done in time for Communion, use another loaf from the bakery for Communion.

Then after you've had your closing, you can wait there until the bread is ready to take home.)

2. Read the Scripture.

Ask:
- What do you think Jesus meant when he said, "I am the living bread that came down from heaven" (verse 51)?
- How does one "eat" the bread of life? (*by living for Jesus*)
- What does the bread of life taste like? (*peace, hope, salvation*)
- What does it mean to feast on the bread of life? (*to have peace, hope, and joy in abundance*)
- What would it mean to be hungry for the bread of life? (*long for God*)

3. Explain that bread is a symbol of the food we need in order to live. When Jesus talks about being the bread of life, he is using an image of something needed to sustain life and saying that he is all that is needed for eternal life.

Ask:
- Are you feasting on the bread of life, or are you famished by a lack of bread?

4. Allow fifteen to twenty minutes for silent reflection. Bring paper for the youth to journal if they want, or they can just spread out and sit quietly. Tell them to reflect on the previous question and listen for God's voice. When they are done, gather them together for Communion.

5. Have a clergy person offer Communion, using the bread that your group just baked. If a clergy person is not available, celebrate with a love feast. Simply lay the loaves out on the table and serve grape juice with the bread. Either way, make sure the youth get a large piece of bread and have their fill.

6. Reread verse 35. Explain that Jesus gives us all that we need for living. He is our spiritual nourishment. We don't need to desire anything else because Jesus is our all.

7. In closing, ask the group to form a circle. Place a plate with a loaf of broken bread on a chair in the circle. Tell the group that it is a symbol of Christ's presence with you. Explain that Jesus draws our hungry souls unto him. Close in prayer. As a benediction, ask youth to say "be filled with the bread of life" to one another, then feast together on the leftovers.

DESTINATION  Banquet—

Focus: Youth will link the feasts and banquets in their lives with Jesus' teachings about the kingdom of heaven and who's invited to the banquet table.

Scripture: Luke 14:7-24

Location: A banquet

J esus' teachings around the banquet theme include wise advice, instruction, and a parable. Youth enjoy a good meal. Why not bring the two together by throwing a fancy banquet for your kids and then bring in this Scripture as a way of firming the experience in their minds, creating a link between the Scripture and a wonderful feast?

Even though the banquet may be at a regular meeting time, try sending out invitations for this particular program. About two or three days ahead, ask each youth if he or she can make it to the banquet. Show youth that you are very interested in their attending.

Make the banquet fancy and elegant, if possible. Set the table beforehand, using a tablecloth, nice dinnerware, silverware, and glasses. For an added touch, try some flowers, candles, and asking the guests to dress up for the event. Get them curious about what you have planned. You can hold the banquet in a banquet hall, someone's home, or even your church fellowship hall. As with anything, make adjustments to suit your youth group. You will need to recruit adult volunteers to cook and serve the meal following the program.

On the way:

Have the youth arrive at the normal meeting place and then continue as a whole group to your destination, bringing everyone to the banquet at the same time. Talk with the youth as you travel about the most important event to which they've ever been invited. How did people celebrate?

At the site:

1. Invite the youth to sit around the table. Thank them for coming and tell them you are going to begin by reading a Scripture. Tell the youth that the Scripture tells of a time when Jesus was invited into the house of a prominent Pharisee—a leader in the community. Jesus taught, even then, how one should conduct oneself at a party.

2. Read Luke 14:7-11.

3. Ask:
- In what ways did Jesus humble himself in life?
- What does Jesus mean when he says, "For all who exalt themselves will be humbled, and those who humble themselves will be exalted" (NRSV)?

4. Read Luke 14:12-14.

5. Ask:
- If you were a guest at this party, what would you think of Jesus' advice?
- If you were the host, what would you think?
- What would happen if you were to take Jesus' advice for the next party you throw?
- How would your own friends react?

6. Read Luke 14:15-24.

7. Explain that Jesus is referring to the Jews—God's chosen people. They were offered the kingdom of heaven through Jesus, but many turned down the invitation. God then invited the outcasts, the Gentiles who did not know God, to the kingdom. Tell the youth that the parable can be applied on a more personal level, too.

Ask:
- How can you relate this story to your own life and experiences?

8. Ask:
- What are some excuses you use in order to get out of going somewhere you do not wish to go?
- What excuses have you used for not going to worship? for not studying God's Scriptures? for not praying at a time when it was needed?

Notes

_____

_____

_____

_____

_____

_____

_____

_____

_____

_____

_____

_____

_____

_____

9. Point out verse 20 where the excuse was, "I just got married, so I can't come" (NIV).

Ask:
• Was this a good excuse for not coming to the banquet?

Explain that while there may be perfectly legitimate excuses that would cause one to think twice about coming, the banquet with Christ is always more important than any other engagement.

10. Tell the youth that the kingdom of heaven is like a huge banquet with the finest foods and china. Each of them has been invited. They must think about how they choose to respond. Tell the youth that the benefits of this banquet have already begun. We who answer yes to the invitation need not wait to die before we enjoy that kingdom-of-heaven banquet. Jesus has invited us now, and the party has started. One way the banquet can be enjoyed is through the fellowship of those who have answered the invitation already—the community of faith.

11. Begin the meal after a prayer, thanking God for this gathering of disciples whom God has brought to this banquet.

12. After the meal, discuss how the youth are feeling.

Ask:
• How did it feel to be treated so specially?
• What insight does this experience give you about Jesus? about what God desires for us? about who is welcome at the banquet table? about how we are to treat others?

13. As a closing, stand around the banquet table and hold hands. Leave a few spaces open to represent those whom the youth will invite to the table. Pray that you would leave from that place changed and moved to invite everyone you know to the banquet.

DESTINATION Beach

Focus: Youth will take time to affirm the group's community, the group's Christ-centered focus, and the group's ministry in the larger community.

Scripture: John 18:15-27; 21:1-19

Location: A beach or lakeshore

One of the unique stories of the Gospel of John is Jesus' breakfast on the beach with the disciples after his resurrection. It's a wonderful testimony of service, love, and community drawn together by Christ and his resurrection. You can bring a memory of community and connectedness to Christ and this Scripture by preparing a breakfast meal for your own youth on the beach.

If you are not near enough to an ocean beach, a lakeshore will do. Try to find a section of beach that is not very populated so there will be no disturbances. Make the program as early in the morning as possible. Before the youth arrive, have everything ready and waiting. You could have the youth meet at the church or someone's home first. Then they can all come together to the beach and be surprised (as the disciples were) with breakfast. Beforehand, tell them not to eat breakfast before the meeting.

On the way:

If you are able to meet ahead of time and bring the youth to the destination as one group, talk with them about what they like to eat for breakfast. Do they like a big breakfast, a small one, or none at all? Do they usually eat right away when they get up or do they usually get some things done first and then have breakfast? What do they (did they) feel like eating today?

Notes

_____

_____

_____

_____

_____

_____

_____

_____

_____

_____

_____

_____

_____

_____

_____

At the site:

1. Call out to them, "Come and have breakfast!" Greet everyone by name and have everyone sit in a circle around the food.

2. Ask God to bless the food, then hand it out to everyone. Enjoy the meal together.

3. Before reading the Scripture, explain to the youth that the Gospel lesson takes place some time after Jesus rose from the dead. Explain that he had given the disciples instructions to go back to Galilee and wait for him there. They had traveled to Galilee and had been waiting for Jesus to return to them.

4. Read John 21:1-19.

5. Ask:
- Why do you think Peter and the others wanted to go fishing?
- What do you like to do when you just want to "get away" or "be busy"?
- Why do you think Peter jumped into the lake when he recognized Jesus on the shore?

6. Ask the youth if they remember what Peter had done on the night Jesus was arrested. Help them go through the account of Peter's denying Jesus three times. The story is in John 18:15-27. You may wish to read it or help some of the youth retell the story in their own way.

Ask:
- Why did Peter do what he did?
- How do you think he felt after he betrayed Jesus?
- What does it feel like to know you have betrayed a friend?
- What would help Peter know that Jesus forgives him and still loves him?
- What would help you know that Jesus always forgives and loves you regardless of what you do or say?

7. Reread John 18:15-27. Explain that Jesus assured Peter of his calling the same number of times that Peter had betrayed Jesus. Point out that just as the disciples had fasted from eating and would now break their fast with breakfast, so also they were breaking their separation from Jesus. He was spending time with them at breakfast, laughing, affirming them, remembering times spent, and planning times to be spent together in the future. Jesus was still including them in his ministry.

8. Tell the youth that Jesus is still including them—the youth—in his ministry. Jesus wants them to know how much he loves them. He serves them by preparing a meal, a heavenly banquet feast, for them. Explain that your own love for each of the youth is a love from Jesus Christ himself, and that you want them to understand and experience that love.

9. Go to each youth and hand him or her a piece of bread or some part of the meal and say, "I pray that our relationship will nourish you in your faith as you grow closer to Jesus and become a faithful minister of his will in this world."

10. Close with a prayer, asking God to remind everyone of this time spent on the beach.

Notes

DESTINATION

Boat Ride

Focus: Youth will link the story of Jesus and Peter walking on water to their own times of stepping out in faith and trust.

Scripture: Matthew 14:22-33

Location: A boat in water

Much of Jesus' ministry was associated around boats and fishing. Galilee relied on the sea for much of its commerce. It's understandable, then, that some of his teaching and miracles occurred in and around boats. Youth are pretty much a captive audience when they are on boats. There's not much to distract their attention when you're floating out in the middle of a large body of water. Take an opportunity, as Jesus did, to make the experience a teachable moment.

Take the boat out into the middle of the body of water. Also, follow all safety precautions, making sure each person is wearing a life jacket. The program will be more effective if it is done at night, allowing the youth to imagine how it was for the disciples that night.

Bright Idea!

Try this program while enjoying a day at a lake. Just call everyone together right in the middle or at the end of the event and start the program.

On the way:

Prepare the youth for the experience by asking them to tell about a time when they acted out of trust. Then move the discussion towards a question of how they learned to swim. Did they learn? Whom did they trust to teach them? How hard was it? If they have not yet learned, what has been most difficult in learning? How do trust and faith play into learning how to swim?

At the site:

1. Take the boat out into the water. If that is not possible, the program can still be done at the dock.

2. Stop the boat. Make sure everyone can hear. Tell the youth to look out across the water and focus on a point across the water as you read the Scripture.

3. Read the Scripture.

4. Retell the story in your own words, pointing out into the water when the disciples see Jesus walking towards them and beginning to crawl out of the boat when Peter decides to try walking himself.

5. Ask:
- If you were to step out onto the water right now, would you be able to walk on the water? Why or why not?
- What allowed Peter to walk on water at first?
- What caused him to fall?
- Why was he afraid?
- Who are you most like in this story: Peter before he started sinking, Peter after he started sinking, or one of the other disciples who stayed in the boat where it was safer?

6. Explain that we often allow our fears and the worries of this world to take our concentration and focus away from Jesus.

Ask:
- What have you focused on this week?
- How has it stopped you from trusting totally in Jesus?
- How have you brought Jesus into that focus?
- Where do you feel safe?
- What is the storm around you?
- What would it take for you to "step out" of the safety of where you are in your life right now and walk toward Jesus, paying no attention to the storm around you? What would happen?

7. Point out that Peter, when he saw that he was sinking, called out, "Lord, save me!"

Ask:
- What is going on in your life right now that you need Jesus to save you from sinking?

8. Allow a few minutes of silence for youth to really examine their trust in God.

9. Close in a responsive prayer by asking youth to say aloud to God what they need to be saved from and then all responding, "Lord save me!"

For example:
One: From the stress of my final exams …
All: Lord, save me!

DESTINATION  Bonfire —

Focus: Youth will recognize the awesome power of God and learn how God can use us for powerful things when we place our trust in God.

Scripture: 1 Kings 18:16-46

Location: Around a roaring bonfire

The story of Elijah calling down fire from God to ignite the water-soaked wood is a fun story to tell and hear, especially if your group is already gathered around a fire. Use this destination in the fall or winter when it won't be too uncomfortable to be gathered around a hot fire. This program will be most effective if you are familiar enough with the Scripture to tell the story rather than read it.

Make sure your site is in an area where it is lawful for you to have an open fire. If you have to get permission to have an open fire, do so ahead of time. Supply places for the youth to sit around the fire (such as logs, stones, chairs, or a dry place on the ground) within listening range of the storyteller. The fire should be roaring but not so loud that the storyteller cannot be heard. Have a bundle of dry branches nearby for throwing on the fire halfway through the story. Also have some small sticks soaking in a bucket of water for handing to the youth later. Use the bucket of water to put out the fire when you are finished.

Bright Idea! Try planning this destination as a storytelling time around a fire on a retreat. Or consider following this lesson with "Destination Wilderness" (page 137).

On the way:

Ask the youth to tell about a time when they wanted God to show God's power in any particular situation. Have they ever asked God to bring about a miraculous healing or cause something wonderful to happen? Have they ever witnessed some fantastic happening that could only be attributed to God? Think about one or two that you would be able to give as examples. Bring up some awesome wonders we take for granted, such as creation, love, a sunrise, or the birth of a baby.

At the site:

1. The fire should already be going. Begin by roasting marshmallows or singing songs around the fire—anything to get youth comfortable and in the mood to enjoy the time ahead.

2. When you are ready to begin the story and discussion, ask:
- What are some of the signs and actions in the Bible that you have heard when God performed an amazing act that showed God's power? (*Some examples would be the parting of the Red Sea for the Israelites, Jesus raising Lazarus from the dead, David defeating Goliath, and the resurrection of Christ.*)

Tell the youth that you are going to tell them a story of a time when God used fire to show God's incredible power to God's people.

3. Read the Scripture. Better yet, tell the Scripture, expanding on the story by taunting as Elijah did when he told the prophets of Baal to ask their god to ignite the wood. Be sure to explain at first that Elijah had announced a three-year drought to King Ahab that would represent the emptiness of Ahab's worship of Baal.

In all those three years there had been no rain. Already God had shown God's power to the Hebrew people through this punishment for their evil ways. Set up the story by showing the youth how angry the king and others were at Elijah for what God was doing to them. Now, three years into the drought, Elijah returns to humiliate the prophets of Baal and show God as the Supreme Ruler.

4. Ask:
- What things in the story had the most impact on you? Why?
- What thoughts did you have about the story as it was being told?
- Why do you suppose Elijah had the people put so much water on the wood and the offering?
- How would you have responded if you had seen fire fall from the sky and burn up the sacrifice, the wood, the stones, and the soil and dry up the water in the trench (verse 38)?

5. Remind the youth of some of the miracles they had mentioned before you gathered at the fire. Point out that Elijah, out of trust and obedience to God, arranged for a way that God's glory could be seen among many unbelievers.

Ask:
- In what ways do you allow God to use you to show God's glory to many people?

Notes

_____

_____

_____

_____

_____

_____

_____

_____

_____

_____

_____

_____

_____

_____

_____

_____

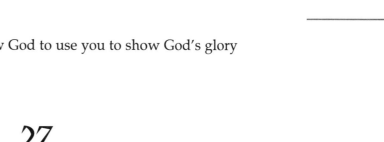

• What convinces you most about God's power and presence in your life? miracles? God's Word? what others tell you? your own experiences? your own changed life?

6. Explain that, above all, God wants to have a closer, more loving relationship with us. God wants us to recognize God's power and might, but God also wants us to experience love and grace—the most powerful gifts of God. At times in the Scriptures God sees the need to show power through miracles like this one from First Kings. In fact, the Old Testament tells us that God showed power through miracles over and over again to the Hebrew people. They repented and changed their ways for a time, but soon they were up to their usual antics again. But in God's miraculous love and grace, God showed the most important miracle—the miracle of Jesus Christ. While we are reminded of God's power and compassion through stories like this one today, we are also reminded that we have access to this power through Jesus Christ. What could possibly keep us from telling others about the power of God's love and grace?

7. As this time by the fire ends, take a soaking stick from the bucket of water and tell the youth that, as with the soaked wood in the story, God can ignite our hearts and lives on fire with faith. It doesn't matter how much we may have soaked down our lives with sin. If we allow God to work through us, God will ignite us so that our own flame burns brightly among all who would see.

Hand out a soaked stick to each youth as you leave, saying, "God wants to ignite your life for God's glory." Have a time of quiet for silent prayer.

DESTINATION

 Bridge

 **Focus:** Youth will see Christ as our advocate, bridging the gap that our sins place between God and us.

 **Scripture:** Hebrews 10:11-25

Location: A bridge

A bridge allows one to travel from one point to another over some obstacle that would normally be a hindrance: a riverbed, a ravine, a canyon, a large body of water or even a highway or railroad. In the same way, Jesus has bridged the gap between human beings and God. He has shown us the love of God and how we should live in response to that love. Meeting on a bridge will help youth recognize the role Christ can play in their life as they seek a closer relationship with God.

Choose a bridge that will not be busy during your meeting time. A footbridge would work very well, since you won't have to worry about automobile traffic. You will also need three carpet squares for every group of ten to fifteen youth.

On the way:

Ask the youth to tell you something they did as a kid that got them into trouble. Talk about what punishment they received when they were in trouble.

At the site:

1. Gather the group on one side. Divide into teams of ten to fifteen. If your group is fewer than fifteen persons, stay together. Tell the teams that they are to try to get to the other side of the bridge using only three carpet squares. (Make the beginning and the ending of the bridge the start and finish lines.) The youth must get their entire group across the bridge and can only be standing on the squares. If any fall off the squares, that group must start over again. If you have more than one group, you can do this as a race to reach the other side first.

 **Bright Idea!** This particular program could be something you could "throw in" on a long road trip. If you are ahead of schedule and your group needs a break, pull off the road near a bridge and begin the program.

Notes

2. Once all groups have reached the other side of the bridge, ask:
- What was the goal in this exercise?
- What made it most difficult to reach that goal? Why?
- What made it easier?
- What did you use in order to reach your goal?

3. More than likely, the youth did not mention the bridge in their answers. The way you worded the directions of the game perhaps caused them to simply take the bridge for granted, when, in fact, the bridge was one of their biggest aids in achieving their goal (to get their whole group to the other side). Keep this in mind as you lead the following discussion.

4. Explain to the youth that Christ is like our bridge to God. Paul states that our sins—any and all of our sins—have separated us each from God. Only through God's grace and faith in Jesus can we find salvation.

Ask:
- How is our separation from God similar to this destination?
- In the game, what allowed you to reach the other side?
- How, then, is Jesus like a bridge?
- What does Jesus span so that we can reach God through him?

5. Read the Scripture. Explain that the Jewish priests believed that certain actions—sacrifices—would take away their sins and make them pure and perfect.

Ask:
- What kinds of things do we do to try to take away our sins?
- Thinking of those things and our struggle to become perfect, what does it feel like to hear from verse 14, "For by a single offering [Jesus] has perfected for all time those who are sanctified" (NRSV)? (Explain that the "sanctuary" that we are to enter with confidence in verse 19 refers to our salvation. Paul is referring to the fact that through Christ, God sees us as perfect, so that we can enter that sanctuary. Sanctification is the process of being made perfect through Jesus Christ.)

6. Point out to the youth that in the game they were to reach the other side as a group.

Ask:
- How is that part of the game similar to how we live out our faith in Jesus?

Reread verses 24 and 25.

Ask:
- Why is it important to be a part of the church?
- Why is it important to help others become part of this "body of Christ" (the church)?
- What do you need to do to help others (your unchurched friends) cross the gap that separates them from God?
- How will you show them the "bridge" that is Jesus?

7. If possible, have the entire group walk to the center of the bridge and lead them in a closing prayer, thanking God for having such love as to bridge the gap of sin that has separated us from God.

Notes

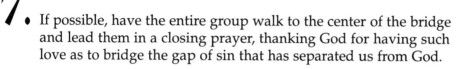

DESTINATION Cemetery

Focus: Youth will connect Paul's words about our resurrection with their own understanding of death and eternal life.

Scripture: 1 Corinthians 15:50-58

Location: A cemetery

Death is not an easy issue to discuss among youth. Often they have an "immortality" complex, thinking "it will never happen to me." When it does happen to someone they know, it can be devastating. All sorts of questions arise that are usually very difficult to answer. Use this program to confront the issues of death and eternal life.

Visit the cemetery you plan to use ahead of time and find the best place to meet with the group. Try to choose an area where many tombstones are in view, where there are interesting epitaphs, and where lights are available if it will be dark. You may want to go to a grave of someone who the youth knew—perhaps a friend who died or a church member. You may need to speak with a caretaker and let him or her know of your plans.

Bright Idea!
This program could work well in a series with "Destination Funeral Home" (page 60), allowing your youth to develop some comforting and helpful experiences around the topic of death.

On the way:

As you are traveling to your destination, ask the youth to come up with some creative epitaphs that they would like on their tombstone when they die. You might suggest a few humorous or creative ones in order to get things started.

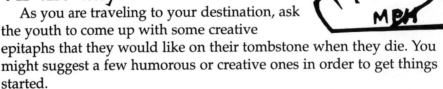

Ask:
• If you were to die tonight, what do you think your tombstone should/would say?

At the site:

1. Tell the youth to find a partner and spend the next five minutes looking at the tombstones. Have them look for someone who was born closest to their own birthday, someone who died at about the same age as they are, and someone with the same name (first or last)

as theirs, and a unique epitaph. Blow a whistle or horn (or flash lights) when it is time for them to return to the meeting place.

2. Ask the youth to talk about what they found on their scavenger hunt through the cemetery.

Then ask:
- What did it feel like, walking among the tombstones?

Talk for awhile about the different feelings and thoughts experienced.

3. Ask:
- What do you think happens after a person dies?
- Why do you think that?

4. Read the Scripture.

5. Ask:
- What is Paul saying happens after a Christian dies?
- What do you think Paul meant when he wrote verse 57: "But thanks be to God, who gives us the victory through our Lord Jesus Christ" (NRSV).
- If there is no death, then what does it mean that all these people still died?

6. Explain that because Jesus died and then rose from the dead, any who accept him as their savior will also be raised from the dead so that they can live with him eternally.

Ask:
- When you get to heaven, is there someone there who you'd like to try to find right away? Who? Why?

7. Try to get the youth to look at their own mortality.

Ask:
- Do any of you know someone your own age who has died?
- How close were you to him or her?
- How did he or she die?

Tell the youth that just because we are young or strong or even Christian does not mean that we are spared from the death of our bodies. God did not create our physical bodies to be immortal.

Ask:
- What would living be like if you thought you would only live here and never have an eternity with God?

Notes

_____

_____

_____

_____

_____

_____

_____

_____

_____

_____

_____

_____

_____

Notes

• How would things be the same?
• How would things be different?
• Do you know someone whom you want to live eternally with God?
• How could you tell him or her the good news?
• How will he or she receive it?

8. Remind the youth that Jesus said that he came into the world so that each of them might have abundant life. One way he gives us a full life is by assuring us that we need not worry about death. It is not permanent. We will spend eternity with God.

9. As you close, invite the youth to look out over the cemetery and imagine what it will be like when all those who have died will be resurrected. Read verses 52-55 again and close in prayer.

DESTINATION

Clay

Focus: Youth will link the action of molding images out of clay with God's loving creation of them as individuals.

Scripture: Genesis 2:4b-8

Location: Tables with clay at a person's home or craft shop

The image we receive from the creation story of God forming the first human out of dust and breathing life and spirit into that dust reminds us of whose we are and from whence we receive our own image. Youth, who often have questions and doubts about their self image, can find affirmation and strength in this story when they apply themselves to that creation account.

The essential part of this program is molding clay. Youth will create something of beauty out of something ordinary—just as God created each of us from something as ordinary as dirt. With a little planning, the environment you offer for such an experience can add to the program. Find a place where the youth can sit at tables and concentrate only on their "creations" with no other distractions. A person's house, a fellowship hall, a large room, or even a coffee shop or restaurant (after hours) would work nicely. Many communities have craft shops with workplaces, clay forms, paints, and a kiln available. If you use a craft shop, the youth can spend some time choosing a form to paint, adding their unique touch to their creation and perhaps be more willing to keep that creation. A kiln would allow you to bake the forms once the youth have finished. Youth can pick up their creations later in the week after the clay has been fired or can receive them at their next youth gathering.

Bright Idea! This program could be done as part of a series with "Destination Refiner's Fire" (page 106).

On the way:

Ask the youth what the phrase *to create* means. Talk for a few minutes about things that they have created in their life. What was one of the first creations they remember making as a child? Do they still have it?

Notes

_____

_____

_____

_____

_____

_____

_____

_____

_____

_____

_____

_____

_____

At the site:

1. Have youth sit at the tables while you explain the procedure. Give them at least an hour to create something with the clay. Make sure they have plenty of materials with which to mold. If pre-cast forms are offered, give the youth instructions on how to add their unique touches to those forms with paint. Make sure you and any other leaders spend time mingling with the youth, talking with them about their creations and anything else they may be interested in discussing during that time.

2. At the end of the hour, tell the youth to place a mark on their creation that tells them whose it is. (Initials on the bottom would be fine.) Then invite the youth to wander around the room and look at everyone's creations.

3. Gather the group together in one area and talk about the experience.

Ask:
• What did you like about working with clay?

4. Explain that you brought the group here so that they could experience creating something and talk about the creation story in the Bible. Read the Scripture. As you read, though, read slowly and use eye contact with the youth. When you read verse 7, insert some of your youth's names in place of the word *man*. (Example: "then the LORD God formed Jill and Mark, Maria and Juan, Tim, Monique and Enrique from the dust of the ground. . . .") Look at each of those youth as you read that verse. If you have a large group, don't feel like you need to say everyone's names. The youth will understand your intent and begin to place their name in that list.

5. Tell the youth that God was the first one who created, and when God created, God did so with each of them in mind. God knew at that moment of the first creation that each of them (insert more names here) would be a result of that creation. Just as they each made unique marks on their creations today, God has breathed God's breath into each of them, giving them life and their special qualities. God has a plan for them as individuals, and it is a plan that uses their gifts that have been created by God.

6. Ask:
• Did any of your creations turn out exactly as you had first intended them to be?

Point out that, like our own creation, we at times stray from the way God first intended us to be. That doesn't mean that God gives up on us or sees us as less beautiful. God sees beauty in each of us. Regardless of whether our clay "cooperated" with our intentions, the result was still our creation. God has been and still is our creator. God has molded us and continues molding us and shaping us.

Just as the youth placed their "mark" on their own creations, God has placed God's mark on us, claiming us as God's children. God has also breathed God's own breath into our lungs giving us life. If we are drawn to our own creations with which we spent only about an hour, how much more is our loving and perfect creator drawn to us?

7. Give the youth instructions about picking up their creations. Then close with a prayer, asking God to affirm each person present and help them always to understand that God loves them because God created them.

DESTINATION

Focus: Youth will experience what it means for Jesus to be their advocate.

Scripture: 1 John 2:1-6

Location: A courtroom

John says that Jesus is our advocate. An advocate is one who stands and pleads on another's behalf—an intercessor. One example of an advocate is the image of a lawyer pleading a case before a judge. This visit to a courtroom and discussion with a lawyer or judge will help the youth visualize what it means to be an advocate.

Ask church members to recommend a judge or lawyer. Talk to the judge or lawyer ahead of time and ask if he or she can be present for the program. If not, call the courthouse for recommendations. It is most helpful if the judge or lawyer is a Christian who is willing to talk also about his or her faith.

Bright Idea! If possible, try taking the group to an actual court in session, where they can see the work of the lawyers and the judge. If you can arrange it, invite the judge or lawyers to the discussion afterward and give them some time to talk about their own faith and how it guides them in their career.

On the way:

Ask if any youth have ever been to court. Ask them which person they would rather be: the judge, the defense attorney, the prosecutor, or a jury member.

At the site:

1. As you arrive in the courtroom, ask the judge or lawyer to take his or her usual place in the room and ask for a volunteer to take a seat in the defendant's chair. Someone should announce that the courtroom be called to order. Tell the youth that today's "trial" will be to determine if there is proof that the defendant is a Christian. Take a minute to explain to the actors what they will be doing based on the instructions below.

38

2. Spend about five minutes in a mock trial of the volunteer defendant. If you were not able to arrange for a judge, ask for a volunteer judge and prosecuting attorney (if there isn't one present). Do not select someone to be a defense attorney. That role will be explained and filled later in the program. The judge should ask the defendant to offer proof that he or she is a Christian who lives out the faith. The defendant should list some things that sound like good Christian actions. After a minute or two of the defendant's speech, the prosecutor should start listing some "sins" that would counter those "good" acts. Each "good" act should be countered by a "sin." (Of course, all of the "sins" will be made up.)

3. Finally, when it looks like no headway will be made and that the judge may declare the defendant "not guilty" of being a Christian, stand up and interrupt to read the Scripture.

4. Point out that a judge, defendant, and prosecutor are present, then ask:

- What else is needed in this court session?

5. Explain that the Scripture tells us that we have an advocate, Jesus, who stands for us and pleads with us before God, the Judge. Not only does Jesus stand for us as our defense lawyer, but he also makes the atonement (the payment) for our sins.

6. Hand out small pieces of paper and pencils or pens and instruct the youth to list those things about themselves that a lawyer might use in order to prove them guilty of being a Christian. Allow about three minutes for the youth to complete their lists.

7. Instruct the youth to turn over their papers and write one word—*sin*—on the back of the pages. Point out that it takes only one sin to draw us away from God's intention for our lives. When we sin, we are no longer worthy of God's kingdom. However, Jesus is our advocate and according to John, he is the atoning sacrifice for the sins of the whole world.

Ask:
- How does it feel to know that you are guilty of a terrible sin but that you have the best defense lawyer who will not only defend you but has also gone in place of you to "do the time"?

Notes

8. Teach the group the words to the hymn, "Jesus Paid It All," which should be included in most hymnals or songbooks. Or you may choose to teach another song about Jesus' debt that is familiar to your group. Sing it together.

Ask:
- If Jesus pays our debt and stands for us to defend us for all we do, what is your response?

9. Reread verses 3-6.

Ask:
- What do you need to do in order to walk closer to the way that Jesus walked?

Tell the youth to write their answers (or circle them, if they are already written) on their papers. Then ask them to circle three things on their papers that they will work on in the next month so that they can walk in God's truth.

10. Close with prayer of thanksgiving that we have an advocate in Christ Jesus.

DESTINATION  Crosses on a Hill

Focus: Youth will examine the physicality of Jesus' death on the cross and consider their commitment to following him.

Scripture: Luke 23:26-49

Location: Three crosses on a hill

Often in the countryside one will pass by a hill where three crosses are standing. Some of these have been standing for years, reminding travelers and passers-by of the sacrifice that Jesus made for us all. If one of these sites is not available to you, you might create your own. Choose a place where you can park and walk to your site, if possible.

This destination lends itself to a Palm Sunday or special Good Friday outing but can be used any time.

On the way:

Ask the youth to talk about what would cause them to change their minds about someone they loved. Try not to let on that they are going to look at what Christ encountered on the day he was crucified, but help them to begin seeing how quickly an opinion about someone can change. This discussion will help the youth understand how the crowd was swayed from praising him on Palm Sunday to calling for his crucifixion a week later.

At the site:

1. Before you walk up the hill, ask the youth to imagine themselves walking to the place of the cross on the day Jesus was crucified. When you arrive at the foot of the crosses, invite them to touch a cross, to knock against it, to feel its sturdiness and roughness, to imagine carrying it, being nailed to it, and being hung on it.

2. Read the Scripture from Luke 23:26-49. Try reading the text from a version like *The Message* or the Contemporary English Version of the

Bright Idea!
If you're on a long trip and happen to pass by one of these locations where three crosses are standing, try spontaneously stopping and doing this program. It will be a surprise stop, but often God's Spirit comes to us in surprising times and places.

Bible. The reading should be slow enough for the youth to envision what happened.

Option: You may read the following graphic description of the pain and brutal suffering of the death that Jesus encountered when he was crucified. Then move into the questions.

"[The cross is placed] on the ground and . . . [the exhausted man] is quickly thrown backward with his shoulders against the wood. The . . . [executioner] feels for the depression at the front of the wrist. He drives a heavy, square, wrought-iron nail through the wrist and deep into the wood. Quickly he moves to the other side and repeats the action, being careful not to pull the arms too tightly, but to allow some flexion and movement. The . . . [cross] is then lifted . . . [into] place. . . . The left foot is pressed backward against the right foot, and with both feet extended, toes down, a nail is driven through the arch of each, leaving the knees moderately flexed. The victim is now crucified. As he slowly sags down with more weight on the nails in the wrists, excruciating, fiery pain shoots along the fingers and up the arms to explode in the brain—the nails in the wrists are putting pressure on the median nerves. As he pushes himself upward to avoid this stretching torment, he places his full weight on the nail through his feet. Again there is the searing agony of the nail tearing through the nerves between the metatarsal bones of the feet.

. . . As the arms fatigue, great waves of cramps sweep over the muscles, knotting them in deep, relentless, throbbing pain. With these cramps comes the inability to push himself upward [to breathe]. . . . Air can be drawn into the lungs, but cannot be exhaled. Jesus fights to raise himself in order to get even one small breath. Finally, carbon dioxide builds up in the lungs and in the blood stream and the cramps partially subside. Spasmodically, he is able to push himself upward to exhale and bring in the life-giving oxygen. . . . Hours of this limitless pain, cycles of twisting, joint-rending cramps, intermittent partial asphyxiation, searing pain as tissue is torn from his lacerated back as he moves up and down against the rough timber: Then another agony begins. A deep, crushing pain deep in the chest as the pericardium slowly fills with serum and begins to compress the heart. It is now almost over—the loss of tissue fluids has reached a critical level—the compressed heart is struggling to pump heavy, thick, sluggish blood into the tissues—the tortured lungs are making a frantic effort to gasp in small gulps of air. . . . He can feel the chill of death creeping through his tissues. . . . Finally he can allow his body to die. . . . "

Reprinted from "The Crucifixion of Jesus," by C. Truman Davis, M.D., in *Arizona Medicine*, March 1965, pages 183–187.

3. When the reading is over, ask:
- When have you been punished for something you didn't do?
- How did it feel?

- Have you ever taken someone else's punishment? Why?
- Do you know persons who wear the symbol of the cross?
- What does it mean to them?
- What does it mean to you?

Help youth make the connection of Christ taking our punishment on the cross. Take your time asking the questions and give them time to think about their answers. Help them really consider what the symbol of the cross means to them.

4. Take your time with the following questions. Youth don't get enough silent time to examine their hearts. Let this be a time of quiet examination for them. Ask the questions, then, when you feel they're ready, ask volunteers to discuss their answers.

Ask:
- When Jesus said, "Father, forgive them" who was he asking God to forgive?
- When did the death of Christ on the cross take on personal meaning for you?
- If you were about to die, how confident would you be that you would be with Jesus in paradise? Why?

5. Ask the youth to form a circle around the cross and kneel. Give them an opportunity to pray silently. Encourage them to be still and listen for what God wants them to hear. As a closing, invite them to rise and sing (or have someone sing as a solo) "Were You There." If this is not a familiar hymn for your group, sing a related song they know. Ask everyone to walk back to the vehicle in silence.

DESTINATION  Crossroads

Focus: Youth will link the crossroads with their decision to follow Christ and determine where they are along the journey of discipleship.

Scripture: Matthew 4:18-22; Jeremiah 6:16

Location: A crossroad intersection

The image of a crossroads suggests a multitude of ideas and examples for any youth meeting. Young people are constantly being pulled in different directions while they face the life-altering decisions of adolescence. The crossroads can help them approach their decisions with a clear sense of making a choice to follow the way of Christ.

Be sure to choose a crossroads that will not be busy during your meeting time. A busy intersection could cause an epidemic of wandering and distraction. The more out of the busy city you can get, the better! If you can, find a crossroads with a yellow caution sign nearby, warning of the intersection ahead. The image on the sign is also the shape of a cross and will be helpful in your discussion. Though the sign might not be available, this program could also be done where two footpaths cross. If you choose to lead this meeting at a footpath crossroads, bring a cross or a picture of a cross to use as your visual for the closing exercise. If possible, bring along a map that shows the particular junction. You will need a copy of "Thy Word." It is on Amy Grant's *Straight Ahead* album and is included in many hymnals. You may also need a battery-operated boom box or someone to accompany the group on guitar.

Bright Idea!

This program could be something you could "throw in" on a long road trip. If you are ahead of schedule and your group needs a break, pull off the highway at a rural crossroads and begin the program.

On the way:

Discuss decisions that the youth have recently made. Ask the youth to think of any decision they have made that changed their lives or an important decision they will be making soon. Invite volunteers to tell about the past decision that was life-changing. Adult leaders should also join in the discussion.

At the site:

1. Tell the youth to sit or stand in a group at one of the corners. (If this is a wide footpath or a rural road with no traffic, you might try standing in the intersection itself.) Ask:

- How does this crossroads resemble decision-making?
- How is the choice you may make at this crossroads different from the choices you may make in your life decisions?
- What would help you know which way to go if you came upon this crossroads for the first time?
- What kinds of things give you direction when you come upon a personal crossroads?

2. Show the youth a map with this intersection printed on it. Ask them to find where you are on the map. Have someone describe the kinds of things they see on the map down each road of the intersection.

3. Ask each youth to find a partner. Tell the partners to sit or stand facing each other. Have them discuss their answers from the "on the way" exercise. Then ask the youth to brainstorm, telling their partners one or two likely results of their upcoming decision. If they were to choose one path, what would happen? If they were to choose the other way, what would happen? Give the pairs five minutes to talk about their decisions.

4. Explain to the youth that we will not always know the full impact of the decisions we make. We don't have a map that tells us what is ahead in life. As Christians, though, we do have a type of map that gives us guidance in our decision making. Of course, that map is the Bible. The Bible is God's Word. It guides us in our choices by telling us what is ahead and how to prepare. It also assures us that, no matter what road we take in life, God is there with us.

5. Read Matthew 4:18-22.

6. Have the group examine their level of commitment to following Christ. Tell them to imagine where in this intersection they are concerning their own faith decision.

Ask:
- Are you approaching the crossroads soon?
- Have you reached the crossroads and are standing still, trying to decide if you should follow the road or Christ?
- Have you moved down one road and wish to take a different one?
- Have you chosen to walk with Christ already and are on your way down that road?

Notes

_____

_____

_____

_____

_____

_____

_____

_____

_____

_____

_____

_____

_____

_____

_____

_____

7. Teach the youth the words to the praise song, "Thy Word." It is on Amy Grant's album *Straight Ahead* and is included in many hymnals. As the youth think about where they are along their road of faith, sing "Thy Word" together. You may wish to play the recorded version or ask someone to accompany you on guitar.

8. As a closing, walk or drive to the street sign that warns of the intersection. Ask the youth to look at the sign for a moment. The warning sign for a crossroads is the same symbol for God's decision to choose each of us. The symbol of the cross reminds us that we too have a choice to make. As we encounter decisions to follow Jesus, we will need to choose. (Even not choosing to decide is a decision not to follow.) Our decision to follow Christ is one that will change our lives forever. With Jesus as our guide, we will have help in all our future crossroads.

9. Read Jeremiah 6:16 as a benediction and close in prayer.

DESTINATION

Dark Room — — —

Focus: Youth will understand how their own sinfulness places them in darkness and how Jesus' presence in the world and in their life brings light and life to their darkened world.

Scripture: Psalm 107:10-11; Isaiah 9:2; and John 1:1-13

Location: A dark room

Youth who know Jesus will recognize how God's light has illuminated their own darkness. Those who do not know Jesus will have an opportunity to experience that illumination for the first time. Help your youth respond to the light of Christ in the world as they recognize just what kind of an effect light has on darkness.

Prepare a room ahead of time in order to make it totally dark. Make sure any boxes or furniture are placed so that no one will get hurt while trying to move around in darkness. You will also need a strong flashlight, a lighter, a blindfold for each individual, a candle for each individual, and two large candles.

On the way:

Talk with the youth about what it feels like being in total darkness. Ask them to describe what darkness is like. When you arrive, tell the youth to get into a single-file line. Then, place blindfolds on the youth and ask them to place both hands on both shoulders of the person in front of them. Carefully lead the entire group to the door and into the darkened room. The youth should not know that the room is totally dark yet.

At the site:

1. Leave the door slightly open while you arrange the youth in a circle facing inward, and help them sit down. Remember they are blindfolded, so you will need to place each person where you want him or her to sit.

2. Finally, close the door, closing off all light to the room. Turn on your flashlight and read Psalm 107:10-11 while the youth are still

Notes

blindfolded. Then turn off the flashlight and ask the youth to take off their blindfolds.

3. Ask:
- What is the darkness to which the psalmist is referring in the Scripture? (*being apart from God*)
- How is sin like darkness? (*sin separates us from God who is the Light*)

Explain that the image of darkness is used throughout the Bible to describe people who are living without God.

Ask:
- Why do you think the psalmist and other Scripture writers use this image of darkness?
- How might living without God be like living in darkness?

4. Next, light one of the single, large candles with a lighter and read Isaiah 9:2. Explain that Isaiah was a prophet who foretold the coming of the savior, the Messiah.

Ask:
- As someone who knows what it is like to walk in darkness, what is the message of hope that you hear from Isaiah?
- How can knowing something give you "light?"
- What does light help you find?
- How is this similar to what knowing Christ helps you find?

5. Finally, read John 1:1-13. Hand out candles to each person.

Ask (while passing the flame from your candle on to others around you):
- If you had a lit candle and knew of others who lived in a darkened world because their candles were not lit, would you be willing to light their candles? Why or why not?
- What is it that hinders us from offering the light of Christ to those who don't know him?
- What can help you pass the light of Christ on to those who walk in darkness?
- Who do you know that walks in darkness?
- What will you do to give that person light?

6. End by placing an unlit candle in the middle of the circle and asking youth to pray silently for someone whom they know who does not have the light of Christ in their lives. Then ask them to pray for God to show them how they can ignite a light for that person. Allow some time for silence while youth listen for direction and guidance.

7. Close in prayer.

DESTINATION Emergency Room

Focus: Youth will link an experience at an emergency room with Job's situation and the fact that struggles, discomfort, and even tragedy happen to the good and the bad alike, yet God is always there to bring comfort.

Scripture: Job 1:6-22; 2 Corinthians 1:3-11

Location: An emergency room

The local emergency room is a place where people go in your community for fast help when they need it. Trained people are there who have helped people in extreme pain and suffering. A timeless question humanity has asked is "Why do people suffer?" While this look at an emergency room and Scripture lesson may not answer that question, it will allow your youth to bring up the issue and face how it touches their lives and their faith.

Call the emergency room a week or more in advance and set up your visit. Ask if someone can be there to give you a tour and spend time answering questions. Ask your contact person if a conference room or some sort of area for discussion is available for your group after the tour. If you are not allowed to tour the emergency room, ask if someone could meet with your group to talk about the emergency room experience.

On the way:

Play a game of auto bingo. Here's how: The goal of the game is for each player to complete the spelling of his or her name (first or last, determined before the game begins). A name is spelled by spotting the letters on a license plate, billboard or sign along the road. A player can only claim one letter per source. If another player spots the first letter of a player's name along his or her side of the road, then the player whose name begins with that letter loses all letters and must start all over again.

Letter counts in names vary and some letters are found more frequently than others are. That may seem unfair, but that is also why this game is useful in kicking off the topic for this destination. If there is time, talk a little about what sort of things seem "unfair."

Notes

At the site:

1. Introduce the youth to the representative from the emergency room and allow him or her to take you on the tour. Help the youth feel comfortable asking questions, and try to direct some of the questions or discussions toward how the emergency room team helps those who suffer or are in pain.

2. After the tour and any questions, take the group to the meeting place that you set up ahead of time. Ask the youth to sit where everyone can be seen and heard.

Ask:
- What do you know about pain and suffering?
- What is the worst thing that has happened to you or to someone you know?

3. Tell the youth that you are going to read the beginning of a story in the Bible. The story is about a man named Job, and it comes from a book by the same name. Ask if anyone has ever read Job or if anyone knows the story. Explain that the story begins with a description about Job—a man who is blameless and upright and who pleases God. Then read the Scripture.

4. If time permits, ask the youth to retell the story, and guide them as the story moves around the room in its telling. Help the youth understand just what went on. Then explain that this story is a very old one in which the question is asked, "Why do the good suffer along with the bad?"

5. Ask:
- Have any of you ever wondered, "Why do the good suffer?"
- Did you ever come up with an answer?
- If you were in Job's position and lost everything—all your possessions, all your family, all your health—how would you respond?
- Would you feel angry, sad, depressed, peaceful, or in despair?

6. Tell the group that Job stayed strong in his faith. He never once cursed God or lost faith.

Ask:
- How might tragedy or a crisis actually strengthen one's walk with God?
- Has it ever strengthened yours?
- If so, would you mind telling the group?

7. Several chapters in Job tell of Job's friends giving him some not-so-helpful advice.

Ask:
- If your friend is experiencing some terrible tragedy, what can you tell him or her from your own experience that may help?

8. Read 2 Corinthians 1:3-11, then reread the first two verses again.

Ask:
- What does the writer say is a reason that God consoles us when we are afflicted?
- How good would you be at giving comfort to others if you have never received comfort from anyone—including God?

9. Explain that the book of Job never explains why there is suffering among the "good." God appears to Job and tells him that it is enough to know that God is in control and that God is present in all things. We may never understand why, but we must draw on God's presence and power if we are to exist and survive in a world where there is suffering and hardship.

Ask:
- Why are so many people so willing to come to an emergency room to get physical help but still uncomfortable or scared in coming to God to receive spiritual help in times of tragedy?
- Do you know how to seek spiritual strength and comfort when pain and suffering hit?

10. Close with a prayer, asking God for continued comfort and consolation in all tragedies so that those who receive such comfort can know how to pass it on to others who are also afflicted. Pray also for those in the emergency room and for the staff who treat them.

Notes

DESTINATION Feeding Trough

Focus: Youth will encounter the bleakness and vulnerability around Jesus being found lying in a trough and will ask themselves where they spend time looking for Jesus in the world today.

Scripture: Luke 2:1-20

Location: A feeding trough

The image of a baby lying in a manger has become romanticized over the centuries. We no longer think about the harshness and the vulnerability in which our savior was born. If we think about it, finding Jesus lying in a manger would be much like finding him lying in the sink of a gas station restroom today. To think of the savior of the world humbling himself to be born in such rude circumstances is moving. Bring your youth to a feeding trough so they can see a real example of where Jesus was born.

Find a location where things are not well-lit and the feeling is a bit lonely or removed from the rest of the surroundings. The nativity scene was not the center of attention that first Christmas night. The shepherds had to look for the baby by searching the darkened barns and mangers around the back streets and behind the buildings of Bethlehem.

On the way:

Ask the youth to imagine themselves in the fields around Bethlehem on the first Christmas. Tell them to think of what it would have been like and how they would have responded to the  announcement of the angels. How would their friends have responded when they told them what they saw and heard? Would they continue being shepherds? Why or why not?

At the site:

1. Tell the youth to get out of the vehicle and look for the place where Jesus would be found—if this were the right location in Bethlehem. Wait for them to find it. Some will go right to the manger or feeding trough. Others may not have a clue what *manger* means. Let the

52

Notes

whole group decide just where the place would be and gather around that spot. Ask if they all agree on that spot and why. If the group agrees (and if it is, in fact, the feeding trough), then go on to step two. If they do not agree or if it is not the right spot, then tell them they must keep looking.

2. When the youth have finally agreed on the feeding trough as the location where Jesus would be found if it were the place in Bethlehem, read the Scripture. Read verses 1-7 while standing around the manger (trough). Turn away from the trough and read verses 8-15. Return to face the manger for verses 16-20.

3. Ask:
   • Where would one expect the Savior of the world or the King of kings to be born? Why?
   • What types of people would normally be invited to witness the birth of a king? Why?
   • Why do you think Jesus was born in a manger?
   • What difference did it make that it was a manger with shepherds rather than a palace with special guests?
   • Does it make a difference to you today? Why or why not?

4. If the trough is big enough, have some of the youth lie down in it. If it is not, ask some of them to lie down one at a time in the hay or on the ground nearby. Point out the vulnerability of such a position— out in the open (or in a dirty barn), in the dark of night, a baby, lying in a manger.

   Ask:
   • Why do you think God decided to come first as a baby instead of as a full-grown human being?
   • Why was it important to be vulnerable?

5. Remind the youth that the angels told the shepherds where to look for Jesus. Since Jesus is still alive (and always will be) we can encounter him today in many ways, though some may not be quite so easy as finding a baby in a manger.

   Ask:
   • What or whom does God use today to tell you where to find Jesus?
   • Are the directions God gives clearer or not as clear as those the angels gave to the shepherds?
   • Where have you looked for Jesus in the past?
   • Where would you expect to look?
   • Did Jesus come where he was expected to come on that first Christmas?

Notes

6. Point out that Jesus often shows up in unexpected places. He wants to make himself available to us. That's why he made himself approachable that first Christmas. That's why he made himself vulnerable.

Ask:
- What are some unexpected places that Jesus has shown up in your life?
- What are some unexpected places where you might find Jesus in the next week?
- If the story of the nativity were to happen today in your neighborhood, under what conditions (where, how, when, who would be invited) would Jesus be born?

Allow time for the group to dream and imagine some extraordinary ways in which the Christ might be born in their neighborhoods.

7. Tell the youth that Jesus has, in fact, been born in their neighborhoods and that he continues to come to them each day through other people and through the ways that God's Word is heard.

Ask:
- How can you be more receptive to recognizing where Jesus shows up each day?

Tell the youth that you will pray daily during the coming week that they will not miss Jesus' presence in their lives.

8. Close in prayer. Do what you told the youth—pray for them each day of the week.

DESTINATION

Focus: Youth will link a fishing experience with Jesus' calling his disciples, giving youth and leaders quality time to build on relationships and sharing the message of spreading the gospel to others.

Scripture: Luke 5:1-11

Location: A local fishing hole

When calling his first disciples Jesus said, "Do not be afraid; from now on you will be catching people." Much of Jesus' preaching and ministry was done around fishing villages and with fishermen along the Sea of Galilee. Here is a program that allows youth to experience catching fish so that they can fully understand Jesus' call to "catch people."

Make sure that the place you choose has fairly good results in fishing. Gather the proper equipment: rods and reels, bait and tackle or nets. Net fishing would be most beneficial because it is how the disciples fished. In addition, youth would learn to work together. However, fishing with rods works fine. If you have never fished or do not feel comfortable showing others how to fish, then find a few other leaders who can help some of the youth.

Bright Idea! Try reading the Scripture from a small rowboat or canoe while the youth listen from the dock.

On the way:

Ask the group what it would take for them to give up all they have or all they are doing and follow someone. The disciples gave up their career and time with their families in order to follow Jesus and bring others to him. What would it take for you to be willing to do the same for someone?

At the site:

1. If need be, spend some time showing the youth how to fish. Bring adult volunteers to help those who need assistance. As the youth begin fishing, try to keep them mostly in the same area.

While they fish ask:
• Have you ever fished before?

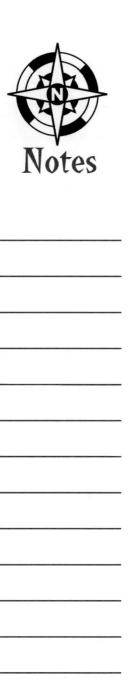
- If so, where is the best fishing spot around here?
- What is the biggest fish you've ever caught?

2. After about twenty minutes, stand along the shore or better yet, out in a boat just off the shore and read the Scripture.

3. Ask:
- What do you suppose caused Peter to fall at Jesus' feet in verse 8 and plead with him?
- Why did he want Jesus to go away at first?
- Why did he decide to follow him?
- Have any of you had a similar response or experience? If so, when?

4. Tell the youth that this is a story of the calling of Jesus' first disciples. Some people can point to a time when they first understood Jesus' calling on their lives.

Ask:
- When is the first time you remember feeling or hearing God calling you to do something?
- What is it that Jesus seems to be calling the disciples to do?
- What does Jesus mean by "catching people"?
- Why is "catching people" so important to Jesus?
- How has he communicated that to his followers?
- How has he communicated that to you?

5. Point out to the group that Peter, James, and John left everything and followed Jesus immediately.

Ask:
- Where is Jesus trying to lead you?
- What is most difficult for you to leave in order to follow him?

6. Explain that this time is probably not the first that these men were with Jesus. Each occasion they had been with him they formed a closer bond and relationship. Jesus wants to do that with each of us, too. He will not ask us to do something until he knows we are ready. If we hear him calling, then he knows we are ready because he is the one who prepared us. Ask the youth to choose one of the metaphors below to describe themselves.

Ask:
- How is your relationship with Jesus now—standing on the shore and watching, learning to cast and bait a hook, stepping out into the water and getting wet, knee deep in a boat full of fish, or I've left it all behind and am close on his heels?

7. Tell the youth that following Jesus means fishing for people. Jesus continually urges his followers to make disciples, that is, bring more people unto him. Encourage them to look for ways they can invite friends to church or youth group that they may come to know and follow Jesus, too.

8. Explain to them that Jesus' call to make disciples is one reason you work with them. Tell them about your call to "catch" them. You want to build on your relationship with them so they will recognize Jesus' call for them as well.

9. Close with a prayer, asking God to help each person hear Jesus' call on his or her life.

Notes

DESTINATION  Foundation

Focus: Youth will understand that having a foundation of faith in life helps us withstand the storms.

Scripture: Luke 6:47-49

Location: A foundation

The foundation you choose could be a number of places. You could visit a building site where only the foundation has been placed, the basement of a very old building where the foundation is made of huge blocks of stone that have been cut from a quarry, or a building that is falling down because of a poor foundation. Consider strengthening the impact by inspecting the foundation of your own church building.

You will also need rocks about the size of a fist or smaller for each individual.

On the way:

Before loading up, ask the youth to attempt a human pyramid. Don't tell them how to do it, just explain that they should use only each other to get one person safely as high as possible. Make sure adults and those who are not part of the pyramid are there for spotting and safety. Once they have built a human pyramid, ask them to carefully disassemble then load up.

At the site:

1. As you stand on the foundation, read the Scripture.

2. Ask:
- Which is a more secure foundation—sand or stone? Why?
- Which is easier to build on? Why?
- What happens when you build on what is easiest?

3. Explain that in Palestine, where things were dry most of the year, a house would stand fine if it were built on sand. When the floods came in the autumn, though, the house would fall or be swept away by floodwaters.

4. Ask:
- What are some "floods" or "storms" that you encounter?
- How have you handled such hardships?

5. Read the lyrics to or sing the hymn "My Hope Is Built."

Ask:
- What does the songwriter find that is so solid about Jesus?
- What can you add to that list?

6. Encourage the youth to examine their faith. Explain that their faith will sustain and strengthen them throughout their lives, and it is the only thing they have that will exist into eternity.

Ask:
- Are you standing firm on your faith or sinking for a lack of it?

7. Hand out the rocks. Tell the youth that the rocks are to remind them that Christ is a solid rock. If they build their lives upon him, they will never be swept away in a storm.

8. Close in prayer.

Notes

DESTINATION  Funeral Home

Focus: Youth will feel more comfortable around those who grieve and understand the effects of death, linking it with Jesus' promise of eternal life.

Scripture: John 11:17-27

Location: A funeral home

Death is often a very uneasy topic for some people. Youth may or may not have experienced the loss of a loved one, but they will certainly have strong feelings about the subject. A visit to a funeral home will evoke some questions and will give the youth some safe, first-hand experience around dealing with loss. Use this program to help the youth feel more comfortable with what happens to a deceased body and with mourning.

Contact the funeral home director well ahead of time, explaining to her or him your plans for the outing. Ask the director if he or she would speak to your youth, telling them what goes on before, during, and after a funeral. If possible ask the director if you can view the room where the bodies are prepared for burial. Explain to your youth, though, that it would be disrespectful to view a dead body, so they should not ask.

Bright Idea! You could use this program in a series with the "Destination Cemetery" (page 32) program as your youth study death and eternity.

On the way:

Ask the youth if any of them have ever been to a funeral. Whose was it? What went on? How did people respond? How would want your funeral to be conducted? (music? clergy? readings?)

At the site:

1. Introduce the funeral director and begin the tour. Make sure there is some time for questions and answers after the tour and presentation. Ask the director about the kinds of things that are said and done in order to bring comfort to the grieved.

2. Move to a private space to begin your discussion. Before reading the Scripture, set it up by explaining that Jesus has arrived at the home of a friend who died four days earlier. Many mourners are present, and the man's sisters are upset because Jesus had not arrived before Lazarus died. Read the Scripture.

Notes

Ask:
- What does Jesus say in this Scripture that gives comfort to the mourners?
- What is the hope that Jesus gives?
- How can Jesus' assurance be hope and comfort for mourners today?

3. Ask:
- Why is it often difficult and awkward to speak to someone who is grieving?
- What kinds of things can you say or do that would bring hope and comfort to people who have just lost a loved one?

4. Explain that part of what it means to be the family of God is that we comfort and support one another when times are difficult. Praying for those who encounter death and loss is an appropriate place to start. Ask the group to brainstorm about ways your youth group can minister to those who have lost a loved one. Create an action plan to care for those in your church who are grieving.

5. Close in prayer by committing your plan to God and asking for the courage to see it through.

DESTINATION

Focus: Youth will be encouraged to plant their faith in fertile soil so that they will grow and flourish.

Scripture: Matthew 13:1-9, 18-23

Location: Local garden footpath or farming field

W hen Jesus told the parable of the sower, many did not understand. The youth may have some difficulty with the parable, too. That's why taking them to a garden path and acting out the parable can help them grasp the wisdom and teaching of the lesson. Any garden path will do, but try to find a garden big enough for the whole group to gather without trampling any flowers or vegetables.

This program would work better in the summer or spring when plants can be visible in the garden. Find or create a path that has rocks, thorns, and good soil nearby. You'll also need a bag full of seed (corn, bean, or pea seed work well, as these are big enough to be seen and to hand out to each youth at the end of the program).

On the way:

Ask the group what they know about planting. Find out if any have ever planted a garden or any kinds of plants. How did it go? What was most difficult? Would they do it again? If any have not gardened, ask what they think about planting and growing and how it would be a challenge if it were something they had to do.

At the site:

1. Gather the youth at the beginning of the garden path. Explain that they should be careful of the plants in the garden because someone is caring for the garden and would not want things crushed.

2. Walk to a place in the garden where stones, thorns or weeds, good soil, and the path are within view. Begin reading the Scripture, starting with verse 1 and reading only through verse 4. As you read verse 4, reach into your bag of seeds and throw out a small handful, making sure much of it lands on the path. Continue reading verses 5 and 6 and throw some seed onto the stones. Read verse 7, scattering some seed near the thorns or weeds. Finally, read verses 8 and 9, tossing some of the remaining seed, but not all of it, onto the good soil. *Note: Use large seeds so they can be easily picked up after the lesson.*

3. Ask:
- What do you think Jesus was talking about when he told this parable?

Give the youth a hint and tell them that the seeds stand for the Word of God. Talk for a few moments about what the youth think the story means.

Ask:
- Who planted the first "seed" of God's Word in your life?
- What happened to it?

4. Continue reading the Scripture, beginning with verse 18. As you read verses 18 and 19, show the seeds that fell on the path.

Stop and ask:
- What kinds of things hinder you from understanding God's Word?
- How does God's Word get trampled down in your life?

5. Move to the seed that fell on the stones and read the next two verses (20 and 21).

Ask:
- Can you think of a time when difficulties like trouble and persecution have seemed to tear down your faith?
- What kinds of troubles can break down a person whose faith has little root?

6. Continue reading verse 22 and move to the thorns or weeds, pointing out the seeds that were scattered there.

Ask:
- What worries of this life could threaten to choke your ability to hear God's Word for you?
- How can your worries choke off your hearing God's Word?

Notes

_____

_____

_____

_____

_____

_____

_____

_____

_____

_____

_____

_____

_____

_____

_____

_____

7. Finally, move to the good soil, point out the seeds that fell there, and read verse 23.

Ask:
- What makes this location different from all the rest?
- Why does God's Word bear fruit when it lands in good soil?
- What is "good soil" for God's Word to grow in?
- How can you offer good soil for God's Word to take root and grow?

Explain that the good soil is connected to the one who hears God's Word and understands it.

Ask:
- What kinds of things will help you to understand God's Word better?

8. Ask:
- Which of the four places best describes how God's Word is being received in your life right now?
- What do you need to do to develop stronger and deeper spiritual roots in your life right now?

9. Gather the group in a circle in the garden and ask the youth to tell about something that is attempting to "choke out" God's Word in their lives. As each person tells a little about his or her concerns, say a short prayer for that person. At the end of the prayer, hand each person a seed. Explain that the seed is a reminder that God's Word is coming to the youth each day and they are to foster good, fertile soil for that Word to take root and grow.

DESTINATION

Focus: Youth will recognize how a desire to accumulate material treasures hinders us from building our eternal treasure.

Scripture: Luke 12:13-21

Location: Grain elevator

Society preaches, "Whoever dies with the most toys wins," but Jesus taught that "one's life does not consist in the abundance of possessions" (Luke 12:15, NRSV). While most farmers store their crops to sell them in order to provide for others as well as their own needs, the rich fool in Luke's Gospel lives his life out of selfishness and greed. The accumulation of wealth is what is most important to him. Materialism is the message that youth hear so frequently today. Youth are barraged with media hype telling them that they "need" more things, but Jesus' parable encourages all of us by teaching that we can be fully satisfied by storing up heavenly treasures.

Today farmers don't usually store all the food they've grown at their own barns as in Jesus' day. Rather, they take their crops to market and store them at a grain elevator. For your destination, either visit an actual grain or crop storage facility like an elevator or visit the private barn of a local farmer. While the farmer may not store the crops there, the parable does draw us back to the way such storage used to be done.

Speak with the owner of the grain elevator or barn and ask if someone can be present to explain just how much grain or food is kept there, where it goes once it's been stored, and how long the grain is stored.

The purpose of visiting a grain elevator or barn is for youth to see with their own eyes what it looks like to store things. This experience will help them understand the parable a little better, link it to their own lives, and evaluate how much they store earthly treasures whenever they happen by a similar site in the future.

On the way:

Talk about commercials and advertisements. What gimmicks are being used in order to make people believe that they "need" certain items? Ask the youth which

Notes

advertisements work best and why. Talk about how we discern what we truly need and what we just want.

At the site:

1. Ask the youth if they have any idea how food crops such as corn, wheat, or beans are harvested and shipped before they come to the grocery store. Talk about how our food gets to us and if you have brought a farmer or someone with such knowledge to the destination, then ask him or her to inform the group.

2. Explain that in Jesus' day the crops from a farm were harvested, stored, and sold by the farmer. There were no banks in which to keep one's money, and much trading was negotiated with goods rather than on credit or through bank accounts. People would store what was harvested in their own barns, holding it until they needed it or until they could trade it for money or other goods.

Ask:
• How is this system different than today?

3. Read the Scripture.

4. Have the youth determine just what it was that made the man "foolish" in Jesus' parable. Read the Scripture a second time, asking the youth to listen for attitudes or comments that show why the man was wrong in his thinking and in his actions.

5. Ask:
• What does it mean to store up treasures for yourself?
• What does it mean to be rich toward God?

6. Ask:
• What are the most important things to have at your school?
• If you could be popular, rich, or good looking, which would you choose? Why? Are these examples of storing up treasures for yourself or becoming rich toward God?
• From where did the man in the story find meaning for his life?
• Why did that do him no good?
• Where does society today look for security and substance?

7. Explain that the man in the parable has not given his life to God. He cares more about what he has and about relaxing the rest of his days than about his faith or his relationships. Reread verse 21: "So it is with those who store up treasures for themselves but are not rich toward God." Point out that the problem is not that the man stored up treasures for himself. Rather, the problem is that the man focused only on those earthly treasures and cared nothing about the more important treasure—richness toward God.

8. Ask:
- What can you do that will help you store up your treasure in heaven and gain a richness toward God?

9. Help the youth come up with three things they will commit to in the next month that will help them become richer toward God. The youth can choose from this list or come up with some ideas of their own:
- daily prayer
- daily Bible reading
- weekly worship at church
- weekly community service or outreach
- keeping a journal
- fifteen minutes of silence and meditation daily, listening for God
- tithing
- giving up something important (certain types of foods, TV, the telephone, and so forth)
- listening to Christian and other music that is positive
- writing a note of encouragement to someone else daily

10. Close with a prayer, asking God for forgiveness where you have stored up earthly things and neglected godly things. Pray for the strength to surrender the need for "stuff" and gain a longing for God.

Keep track of who made what commitments. In the weeks ahead, talk with youth about the commitments they have made. Find ways to encourage them and help them be accountable.

Notes

DESTINATION  Greenhouse

Focus: Youth will consider what nurtures their own faith to grow while they learn about nurturing plants.

Scripture: Matthew 17:14-20; Mark 4:26-29; Luke 13:18-19; John 4:13-15; John 8:12; John 15:1-4; John 15:16-17; Ephesians 3:16-19; and Colossians 2:6-7

Location: A greenhouse

A visit to a greenhouse creates a variety of images and settings under one roof. Much of what we teach about faith has imagery of planting and growing. In planting something to take home with them, youth will experience nurture and growth. As your youth move around the greenhouse and become familiar with the soil and plants, they will also become more aware of those things that are needed to cultivate a healthy relationship with God.

Make an appointment for a time when the greenhouse is closed to outside customers. Ask the manager if someone from the greenhouse could meet with your group to tell about the procedures of growing plants from seeds and from cuttings. Also, prepare a space for each person to plant a seed or cutting. You will need small planters, soil, seeds, and cuttings. If you cannot get in when the greenhouse is closed, call ahead to find out the least busy time of day you could come in.

On index cards write the following Scriptures and questions. Make multiple cards for each Scripture. Before you begin the program, place the cards in their respective locations based on the instructions below.

- **Matthew 17:14-20.** Questions: How much faith would you say that you have? Is it enough to move a mountain? What mountains have you attempted to move lately? What mountains would you like to move? Have you tried to move them with faith?

  Place this card at the seed rack or table where seeds will be planted.

- **Mark 4:26-29.** Questions: When were seeds of faith first planted in you? Whom did God use to plant them? Who prepared the soil?

  Place this card where there are some plants that are growing well or where soil is stored for potting plants.

- **Luke 13:18-19.** Questions: Has your faith provided care or nurturing for others? Who? Has anyone else's faith provided care or nurturing for you? Whose?
    Place this card among shrubs or trees.

- **John 4:13-15.** Questions: Where do you get water to nourish your faith and make it grow? How do you get it? How often? Is that enough? Are you still thirsty?
    Place this card at a water source.

- **John 8:12.** Questions: How can you walk in the light of Christ? Are you walking there right now?
    Place this card at a light source, either in sunlight or under grow lights.

- **John 15:1-4.** Questions: Is your branch growing, or is it in risk of being cut off? Do you know anyone else whose branch needs a boost of growth? How can you help?
    Place this card among some vines along with pruning shears.

- **John 15:16-17.** Questions: What fruit do you bear?
    Place this card around some fruit plants.

- **Ephesians 3:16-19.** Questions: When have you felt overwhelmed and fed by the love of God? How can a person come to understand the love of God personally? What is God saying to you in this passage?
    Place this card where cuttings are being rooted.

- **Colossians 2:6-7.** Questions: What does it mean to be rooted and built up in Christ? How does the rooting take place?
    Place this card where rooted plants are growing.

On the way:

Ask the youth to think about some firsts in their life: the first time they heard about Jesus' love, the first time they felt God's presence, the first time they had Communion, the first time they made a commitment to follow Jesus, the first time they prayed on their own. Be sure to share some of your own "firsts."

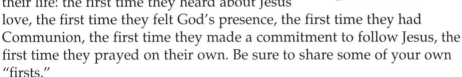

At the site:

1. Have someone from the greenhouse tell the youth about planting and rooting—explaining some of the basics of running a greenhouse. Then show the youth how to do their own planting that they can take home, either a seed or a plant.

Notes

2. Have youth prepare their plants.

3. After the youth have prepared their plants, allow them to move from place to place in pairs. Ask them to read the Scripture cards and tell their answers to their partners. They should find all nine cards. You could have an adult at as many card locations as possible to participate in the conversations with the youth about some of the questions on the cards.

4. When the youth have read all of the Scriptures and talked about the questions, ask them to choose a card that was most meaningful for them or a Scripture that relates to the kind of plant they potted. For instance, if they have planted a seed, they might choose the Mark 4:26-29 passage. If they have planted a cutting or potted a plant, they might choose the Ephesians or Colossians Scripture. When they are done choosing a Scripture verse, have them place the index card on their pots.

5. When the youth have finished, spend some time talking about some of the questions and asking the youth what insight into faith they gained from the images in the greenhouse.

6. Close with a prayer, asking God to continue nurturing the faith of the youth with the water of the Spirit and the light of Christ.

DESTINATION

Harvest — — — —

Focus: Youth will recognize that evil and injustice are very real in this world, but God gives us hope to endure the struggle.

Scripture: Matthew 13:24-30, 36-43; Revelation 21:4-5

Location: A field ready for harvesting

Youth today know (in a very real way) that evil exists. Living with the fact of evil is never easy, but our hope is always found in God who promises to separate the good from the evil at the ultimate harvest time. Use this program to talk about the reality of evil in the world and to discover the miraculous hope we have in God through Jesus Christ.

Prior to your meeting and during harvest season, contact a local farmer and ask permission to hold this program on his or her property. Find a section of field where weeds have crept into the crop. Invite the farmer to talk about farming and what happens when weeds sprout up among the healthy crop. Gather enough stems of the crop to hand out to the youth at the end of the program.

On the way:

Have the youth complete this sentence: "In a perfect world, there would be no more _____." Some youth may give a funny answer while others will take the question seriously. Be sure to accept all answers.

At the site:

1. Walk the youth part way into the field. Ask if anyone knows how the field was planted. If the farmer is present, ask him or her to tell the group a little about the crop and how it is grown. Encourage questions.

If you did not arrange for a farmer to speak to your group, do some minimal research on your own and discuss the basics of farming with the youth: plowing the field, planting the seed, irrigating, and

Notes

harvesting. Get the youth to talk about their knowledge of farming. (It's always best when they can teach each other.) Remember that the point of this lesson is not the growth of the crop, but the process of harvesting—when the crop is gathered and cleaned of the weeds.

2. Point to some weeds in the field and ask:
- Why are weeds in this field?
- How do you think they got here?

3. Tell the youth you will read a parable that deals with evil. Explain that Jesus used this story, not to help us understand why bad things happen, but to help us understand that evil and good exist simultaneously and that God knows the difference between them. We also learn from this parable that at the right time, God will separate good from evil—the ultimate harvest time.

4. Read Matthew 13:24-30.

5. Ask:
- Why does the farmer instruct the servant not to pull the weeds immediately?
- Why is it OK for the reaper to pluck the weeds at harvest time?

6. Read Matthew 13:36-43.

7. Ask:
- What are some of the "weeds" that exist around your life?
- According to the parable, should we destroy weeds around us, or let God be the judge?

8. Explain that Jesus is teaching us that we need not judge nor condemn those evils that try to do us in. We can reconcile and with God's help, love even our enemies, but judgment and condemnation are not our job. Jesus tells us that God will be the ultimate judge at the harvest time. Just as the farmer told the servants not to worry about the weeds and that the reaper would destroy them in the harvest, Jesus tells us not to worry about destroying evildoers in this world. God will judge the good and the bad; the bad will be destroyed and the good will live with God forever.

9. Allow the youth to walk alone through the field examining the growing weeds among the crop. Instruct youth to talk to God about the evils they see around them. Tell them to ask God for hearts focused on the hope of the ultimate harvest time to come, even in the midst of the current evil.

10. After several minutes of time for personal reflection, call the group back together. Pass out some stems of the crop. Tell the youth that when they are afflicted by evil in this world to remember the hope of the harvest time. Be hopeful because of God's perfect judgment and justice. Read aloud Revelation 21:4-5. Close with a group prayer.

Notes

DESTINATION Haunted House

Focus: Youth will learn that the power of God is strong enough to eliminate earthly fears that threaten to consume us.

Scripture: Romans 8:31-39

Location: A haunted house

Youth enjoy getting together around Halloween and visiting a haunted house. These amusement locations have been set up with all sorts of sounds and sights sure to scare your youth. A trip through a haunted house is a night of laughs and fun but can also be a good way to kick off a program on the power of God to drive out fear from our lives.

If you have chosen a commercial haunted house for your destination, make sure your youth know how much money to bring. If you are simply going to a run-down building in your neighborhood, make sure you have permission from the owners. Either way, you should check out the destination before taking the youth, assuring yourself of safety and appropriateness for the program.

Be careful not to bring violence into the theme of the haunted house. Many commercial haunted houses resort to making fun out of violence, something that is not helpful for your youth or this program. Again, visit the haunted house before you take the youth. An easy way to ensure safety is to create your own haunted house in either your own home or your church.

On the way:

Talk about things that the youth fear. Do they fear supernatural beings like ghosts and spirits? Why or why not? Why do they think so many people believe in ghosts and spirits but do not believe in Jesus' resurrection or in God as their creator? Ask the youth to tell about a time when they were frightened the most.

Bright Idea!

If you would like to do this at a time other than Halloween or do not wish to make use of costly haunted houses, then get permission to visit an empty house in your neighborhood. Begin with a few rumored ghost stories people have told about the house and do a walk-through with only a flashlight or a candle. The experience might even be scarier.

At the site:

1. Some youth will be frightened and others will have a no-fear attitude. Try not to get anyone too frightened before entering. Help everyone to see this experience as something fun. Make light of scary things youth will encounter in the house so they see it as humorous. If someone does not wish to go through the house, that is OK. Have an adult stay outside with anyone who does not wish to enter.

2. When the group has finished the tour of the house, gather in a place where there are few interruptions and where everyone can hear.

3. Ask the youth to find a partner and sit facing each other. Have them discuss the following questions:
- What was most frightening in the haunted house? Why?
- What frightens me in real life? Why?

4. Conduct the following survey by asking the youth which number (one to ten) best describes their level of fear concerning each fear listed below. One is no fear and ten is terrified. When you call out the fears below, tell the youth to hold up, with their fingers, the number to which they most relate. Then have the ones clump together, the twos, and so on.

- fear of the unknown
- fear of flying
- fear of clowns
- fear of a dangerous animal
- fear of my own death (painless)
- fear of my own death (painful)
- fear of the death of a close family member
- fear of failing a class
- fear of a friend not liking me
- fear of being classified as "uncool" or "unpopular"
- fear of the death of a close friend
- fear of a commitment

5. Tell the youth that you want them to be able to live life with confidence that God's love is more powerful than anything else. Explain that the Scripture you're about to read assures us that God is stronger than our fears. God is strong enough to drive away all fear.

6. Read the Scripture.

Notes

7. Ask:
  • How much hope does this Scripture give you?

8. Explain that Paul is telling us that Jesus has defeated even death and that God's love is the most powerful force. We have nothing to fear because God's powerful love can overcome all our fears.

9. Ask:
  • What does Paul mean in verse 37 when he says, "We are more than conquerors through him who loved us"?
  • Who conquers our fears and our troubles? How?

10. As a closing, pass out small pieces of paper and invite the youth to write the thing they fear the most on the paper. Then in a moment of silence, ask the youth to pray that Jesus would conquer their fears. When they have finished praying, instruct them to rip up the paper into as many pieces as possible and as they throw the bits of paper into the garbage, tell them to assertively say, "I am more than a conqueror against my fears because of Jesus Christ."

DESTINATION

Hill

Focus: Youth will experience a time of silence and solitude to examine how much time they spend listening in prayer.

Scripture: Mark 9:2-10

Location: A hill or mountain

H ills and mountains were viewed as holy places and places of personal retreat in the Old and New Testaments. God made his covenant to Noah on the mountain after the ark had settled. God spoke to Moses through the burning bush on Mount Sinai. Moses sought God's commandments on that same mountain. God sent Abraham to a mountain to sacrifice Isaac. The temple of God was built on the Mount of Olives. Jesus gave many sermons from mountains.

In this program youth are taken to a hill or mountain to learn about the time when Jesus took three of his closest disciples onto a mountain and was transfigured before their eyes. During that time, the disciples heard God proclaim about Jesus, "This is my Son, marked by my love. Listen to him" (verse 7b, *Message*). As the youth spend this time on the mountain they will also be given a lengthy time of silence and solitude in order to experience listening to Jesus.

This program works best with only a few youth so that during the quiet time, each youth can go to a place alone and not see or be seen by other youth. The spot on the mountain or hill to which you choose to take your group should be a quiet place of few people. If you are hiking, make sure that you are allowing enough daylight after the program that everyone can safely walk back down the hill.

On the way:

Ask the youth to tell about times when they have climbed a mountain. Talk about a time when they felt especially close to God.

Bright Idea! Consider climbing to this destination. Along the way you can talk about how often in the Scriptures people went to the mountains to seek time alone with God.

Notes

_____

_____

_____

_____

_____

_____

_____

_____

_____

_____

_____

_____

_____

At the site:

1. When you reach the top of the mountain or hill and find a place that is fairly quiet and out of the way of crowds or onlookers, ask the youth to sit together in a place where they can hear and see you.

Ask:
- Why do you suppose people often associate mountain tops with seeking God?

2. Tell the youth that you are going to read a story from the Scriptures about a time when three of Jesus' disciples felt very close to God on the mountain top. In fact, they even heard God speak to them.

3. Read the Scripture. (Read from two or three different versions of the Bible, including *The Message*, if possible.)

4. Ask:
- What do you think the disciples felt or thought when Jesus invited just the three of them with him to the mountain? when they saw Elijah and Moses talking to Jesus? when they heard God's voice speaking to them?

5. Tell the youth to break into pairs and discuss the following questions:
- Who has had the biggest spiritual influence in your life? How?
- When have you felt especially close to God?

6. Tell the youth that this story is called the Transfiguration. Ask if any of them know what *transfiguration* means. The transfiguration of Jesus means that Jesus' glory was seen and heard, even experienced by others on that mountain.

Ask:
- Have any of you ever seen or heard Jesus' glory being revealed to you?

Explain that God wants each of us to experience such glory when we are ready in our walk with God. God told the disciples, "This is my Son, marked by my love. Listen to him" (verse 7b, *Message*)."

Ask:
- How do you go about listening to Jesus?
- How much time do you spend in silent prayer, just listening?

7. Tell the youth that you are going to give them some time to sit alone in silence with God. All they are asked to do is listen. If they want to talk to God, they may do so, but most of the time spent should be in silence, listening for God's words or guidance. Explain that God speaks to us in many different ways: through Scripture, through the counsel of others, through our own thoughts and dreams, and in nature. Tell the youth that as they listen in this time they should try to discern if the thoughts and ideas they have might be from God. Allow twenty to thirty minutes of silence.

Notes

8. After the quiet time, talk about the experience. Bring everyone back together and offer some time for the youth to discuss what they felt, saw, and heard.

Ask:
- Was this hard or easy?
- Is a long time of silence easy or hard to schedule into your life? Why?
- What did some of you hear, see, or feel?
- Could God be talking to you in any of those things?
- How can you know if something you feel is God speaking to you?

9. Tell the youth that Scripture is a good testing ground for our conversations with God. If God is telling us something, it will not go against Scripture. Encourage the youth to talk with someone they trust and whom they believe is close to God when they try to discern a message from God.

10. Close with a prayer, asking for a more attentive ear to hear and a heart to understand God's Word.

DESTINATION  Hot Fire—

Focus: Youth will understand that the need for the church in their spiritual lives is similar to the need a hot coal has for the rest of the fire if it is to stay hot.

Scripture: Ephesians 4:1-16

Location: A campfire, around a wood burning stove, a fireplace, and so forth

A bed of burning, hot coals will remind the youth that they need to be associated with a community that is "on fire" for God, giving them fuel for their faith as they grow. A simple campfire would work for this program, but any fire will do. The fire should have been burning for awhile, though. There should be a bed of red-hot coals before beginning the program. You will also need something with which to safely take a hot coal out of the fire.

Bright Idea!

"Destination Hot Fire" is best used with mature believers. Try it during a leadership retreat.

On the way:

Talk with the youth about the church. Tell them why you have found the church important. Tell them what drew you to your church and how you see God at work there. Talk about some of the individuals in the church who have strengthened you along your faith walk. The way you tell about your own thoughts and feelings during this time will shape the youth's discussion later.

At the site:

1. When everyone has settled down into a place by the fire and the hot coals have started becoming plentiful, make sure you have the youths' attention as you take a hot, glowing ember from the center of the coals and set it safely away on a stone. Set it close enough to the fire that it can be seen, but not so close that it receives heat from the fire.

2. Ask the youth to talk awhile about their own experiences with their church.

Ask:
- What do you like about your church?
- What do you not like about it?
- How do you see God at work in your church?
- How is the church at work in your life?
- Who in the church has given you strength in your faith? How?

3. Tell the youth that you will be reading a Scripture from Paul's letter to a church in Ephesus—an ancient congregation that existed when the church was very young. Explain that Paul was giving advice to the church on what was important. Tell the youth to listen for instructions that speak specifically to churches as you read.

4. Read the Scripture.

5. Ask:
- What directions does Paul give to the church?

6. Reread verses 15 and 16. Explain that when Paul is using the term *the whole body* he is talking about the church. The church is the body of Christ: his hands and feet and voice in the world.

Ask:
- How can the church be, as Paul puts it in verse 16, "joined and knit together by every ligament with which it is equipped, as each part is working properly"?
- A healthy body "promotes the body's growth in building itself up in love" (verse 16b). How can the church accomplish this? How can you, as an individual, do your part?

7. Explain to the youth that the strength of the church is its diversity. Paul writes in verses 11 and 12 that many have been given different gifts "in order to equip the saints for the work of ministry, for building up the body of Christ." The intention of the church is to use its diversity in building each other up so that we can continue carrying out Christ's work in the world.

Ask:
- What is the benefit of doing Christ's work in the world as a part of a group rather than of an individual who is not working as part of a group?

8. By this time the coal you set aside should be somewhat darker than the other coals that are still in the fire. Draw attention to the lone coal.

Notes

Notes

_____

_____

_____

_____

_____

_____

_____

_____

_____

_____

_____

_____

_____

_____

_____

Ask:
- How is this coal and what happened to it similar to one who attempts to do God's work alone in the world, without the support and community of the church?

Allow time for the youth to talk about the similarities. Help the youth come to the realization that being involved in a church is important in the growth of our faith, in our worship, in our development as disciples of Jesus Christ, and in our ministry and calling to the world.

9. Place the darkened coal back in the fire. As you watch it regain its glow, invite the youth to think about those they know who need the warmth and support of a congregation. Encourage them to do what they can to bring those individuals back into the "warming fire" of the church. Encourage the youth to talk with you about ways in which they feel called to serve in the church.

10. Close with a prayer, asking God to light a fire among your leaders, your group, and in your church. Pray for the strength and courage to boldly do the work of Christ in the world.

DESTINATION Jailhouse — — —

Focus: Youth will link the experience of being in jail with our being bound by sin and Christ's freeing us from that bondage.

Scripture: Romans 8:1-2

Location: The county or city jail

The Bible is full of stories and images of being in jail. Joseph was in prison for something he didn't do. John the Baptist was held in prison for saying things others didn't want to hear, as were Paul and Silas. Jesus even said of those who are in prison, "When I was in prison, you visited me." This lesson is centered on Paul's text, but you could use any other "jail" Scripture. (You may wish to use this location for a Bible study on one of these stories, as well.)

You will need to call ahead in order to make sure the police or sheriff will allow you to bring your group for a lockup lesson. Ask one of the police officers to tell about the experience of being in jail. (Or you could have a prisoner already "planted" in jail who will tell the group what it's been like for him or her to spend time in that jail.)

Depending on the size of the jail, you may wish to do this with a small group of youth. This program works best when there are not too many people in the jail cell at once. Help the youth get a feel for what it's like being locked inside a cell. Everyone should get a chance to be "locked up."

On the way:

Ask the youth to think about a time when a lie may cause them to get "stuck" in a series of more lies. Most likely many youth will be able to remember a time when they or someone they know has lied, only to find that they had to tell even more lies in order to avoid being caught. Ask them if they think it's possible to become controlled by lies. As you travel to the site, discuss some of these instances or make up a "tall tale" of your own that is a good example of one lie leading to another and another.

Bright Idea!

For an added twist, invite some off-duty police officers to come and interrupt your meeting by arresting the whole group and taking them down to the police station. They can go through a "booking" procedure and be locked in jail, where you can begin the program.

Be *very sure* you have informed the parents beforehand.

Notes

_____

_____

_____

_____

_____

_____

_____

_____

_____

_____

_____

_____

_____

_____

_____

At the site:

1. When you arrive at the site, don't say too much. Simply speak quietly to the jailer and ask everyone to step into a cell. If allowed, close the door. Then begin by having the jailer, one of the police officers, or the sheriff (or your "plant") tell what an average prisoner experiences in jail.

2. Ask the youth:
- What do you think it would be like to be in jail?
- What would you miss the most?
- What kinds of things would you think of while you were imprisoned?
- Do you think God intends for people to have to spend their lives in jail? Why or why not?
- What do you enjoy about freedom?
- What kinds of things take away your freedom in life?

3. Read the Scripture.

4. Ask:
- How can living in sin be similar to being in jail?
- How is it different?

5. Explain that when we sin we allow something else to take away who we are meant to be. God did not create us to be sinners. Rather, we choose sin over what God created for us. Sin, when we live in it and allow it to rule our lives, closes us off from being free and being with God. As we spend more and more time in sin, it is harder and harder to break away from it. We become used to it and forget what true freedom is like. Christ came so that we could be free from our sin and be with God.

6. Have the jailer come and open the door to the cell. Let the cell door swing open, then explain that Christ is the doorway out of sin. Through him we can experience true freedom. Explain that because of God's grace, there is nothing we have to "do" in order to cancel our sins. God's grace in Jesus Christ has already canceled our sins. We are forgiven. We need only accept the gift and live in light of it.

7. Tell the youth that they may leave the jail cell. As they do, one at a time, place your hands on one or both shoulders and say, "Your sins have been forgiven. Christ is with you."

8. Before you load up to return home, gather in a circle and pray together thanking God for the amazing gift of Jesus Christ.

DESTINATION Junkyard

Focus: Youth will learn that they are new creations in Christ, and that God will never see them as less than beautiful, even if the world does.

Scripture: 2 Corinthians 5:16-17

The site: A junkyard

Often, if a person has grown up as a Christian all his or her life, it is not easy to recognize the difference between the "new creation" Paul refers to when we are with Christ and the "old self" before we knew Christ. Those who make a marked change in their lives when they become Christian have the benefit of seeing how Christ has changed them. Help your youth see how Christ has made them new (and how he continues to make them new) by this visit to a junkyard.

Look for a junkyard that has a variety of objects available. An old auto junkyard will do if none other is available. Call ahead to tell the owner you're coming, and write a note of thanks to the owner sometime in the week following the visit, explaining to him or her how the visit helped the youth to understand how Christ makes us new creations.

You will also need a copy of *The Velveteen Rabbit*, which should be available in your local public library.

Be sure to be extra safety-conscious. Caution youth not to pick up any items that are stacked in such a way as their removal might cause other junk to fall.

On the way:

Ask the youth about the things in their lives that make them feel worthless or that take away their self-esteem. Even the most confident young person has times when his or her self-esteem is being eaten away by something or someone. If you can get your youth to share some of these times, then they will be well prepared for the program.

Notes

_____

_____

_____

_____

_____

_____

_____

_____

_____

_____

_____

_____

_____

At the site:

1. Play "Liar's Club." Tell the youth they have five minutes to find an odd object that they think no one else will recognize. They must bring that item back to the group, or take the group to the item, and tell the group what that item is. They may make up their explanations. In fact, encourage them to do so. The more bizarre, the more fun. Others can also give their own explanation of the item's purpose. When four or five explanations have been heard, the group must vote on which one is the true use of the item.

2. Find something old and broken down that everyone recognizes: an old car, an old bike, or an old appliance, and gather the group around that item. Ask them to describe the thing you have chosen. Many will no doubt use the negative points in their description: it is rusty, it is broken, it is missing some parts, or it is scratched or dented.

Ask:
- Why do some of our descriptions of things focus on the negative points?
- Do you ever feel like people focus on your negative qualities when they describe you?

3. Point out that the items you've all been looking at are, in fact, old and used. Many are no good anymore.

Ask:
- What would it feel like to be an old item that everyone has discarded to the junkyard?

4. As the youth are thinking about what it feels like to be broken and used, read or tell the story of *The Velveteen Rabbit*. It's about a toy rabbit, used and tattered, that finds out what it means to become real.

Ask:
- How can giving yourself to others make you more "real"?
- When was the rabbit worth the most? Why?

5. Read the Scripture.

6. Explain to the group that it is only God's love for us in Jesus Christ that gives us our worth.

Say:

No one else can determine how much you are worth. Because Jesus died for us all, we are now heirs to his kingdom. When you are in Christ and when you live in his love and allow his love to live through you, then you become a new creature. Your old, sinful self is dead because it has died with Christ. In Christ, we are made new.

7. Tell the youth to find a partner and talk about their answers to these questions:

- What things are different in your life because of Jesus' presence in your life?
- What things would you like to be different still? What is stopping those things from happening?

8. As a closing, make a pile of the junk items the youth gathered. Form a circle around the junk pile and join hands. Pray that God would remind you that you are loved eternally. Thank God for saving you from the junkyard. Ask God to give you confidence as you grow in discipleship. Close the prayer by greeting each other and saying, "Beloved, you are a beautiful child of God!"

Notes

DESTINATION Mall ---

Focus: Youth will connect the experience of walking through a mall with Jesus' instructions to be more concerned about heavenly treasures than earthly ones.

Scripture: Matthew 6:19-21

Location: A mall or shopping center

Most youth love to hang out in malls, so taking your youth to a mall will be like visiting their own turf. This program will cause youth to look at some of the "things" they think they must have and consider Jesus' words about storing up treasures in heaven rather than treasures on earth. It would be good to use many adults for this program. Youth will be prone to wander in a place as familiar as the mall.

On the way:

Ask the youth about some of the things they have. What is their most prized possession? What was their favorite gift ever received? What would they want for their next birthday or next Christmas?

At the site:

1. Tell the youth that they have a half hour to look around the stores and decide how they would spend five hundred dollars if they were told they had to spend it right away. Tell them where and when to meet and make sure the adults in your group split up and go with the youth, giving them a chance to visit during that half hour.

2. When the time is up and the youth have returned, find a good place to meet that is somewhat quiet and away from too many distractions and interruptions.

3. Ask each youth to find a partner with whom he or she did not walk around the mall in exercise number one. Ask the pairs to tell how they would spend their five hundred dollars. After about five to ten minutes bring them back together and ask:

- What was the nicest thing you saw here today?
- Was it worth the price?
- How much would you pay for something you really wanted if you had the money?

4. Read the Scripture.

5. Ask:
- What do you think Jesus meant in verse 20: "But store up for yourselves treasures in heaven, where moth and rust do not destroy, and where thieves do not break in and steal" (NIV)?
- What are "treasures in heaven"?
- Why is a treasure in heaven so much more valuable than an earthly treasure?
- What kinds of earthly treasures do you sometimes spend more time "storing up" than your heavenly ones?

6. Talk for a while with the youth about the things that stand in the way of their heavenly treasures. Help them understand caring more for earthly treasures than God is idolatry.

Ask:
- How can a person enjoy earthly treasures in life yet not get so wrapped up in them that he or she forgets the most important things—heavenly treasures?
- How does one acquire and invest in heavenly treasures?

7. As a closing, walk through the mall one more time with the youth. This time tell the youth to look for something that lasts the longest or has the longest impact. As you leave the mall, stop and ask what item they chose and why.

Then ask:
- How long do treasures in heaven last?
- How can this group help you store up your own treasure in heaven?

8. Before you load up to leave, join hands and pray that God would forgive you for placing earthly things before God. Thank God for being a heavenly treasure in your lives.

Notes

_____

_____

_____

_____

_____

_____

_____

_____

_____

_____

_____

_____

_____

_____

DESTINATION 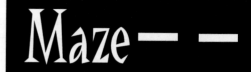 Maze ––

Focus: Youth will learn to relate their own lives to the struggles and decisions they face in a maze and understand how God counsels them in God's way— the right way for their lives.

Scripture: Psalm 23; Matthew 7:13-14

Location: A maze

As youth travel down life's path, they make many turns and choose many directions that soon prove to be the wrong way. Use this program to give your youth an image of such turns and dead ends as they try to make their way through a maze and come to view how God shows them direction along their own life's maze.

Don't be discouraged if you do not know of a maze in your community. If there truly is not one to be found, you can always make one. Before you do that, though, make sure you search the Web for "maze." You might also ask a local newspaper. Often, in communities where some of the popular crops are between five and ten feet tall, farmers will cut a maze in their fields. If you do not know of one of these then perhaps a nearby farmer would be willing to cut a small one in a field for your group.

Another way of making a maze is by either forming one in a fellowship hall or gym out of cardboard or by drawing a very elaborate one on the floor out of tape. You can find patterns for mazes in a puzzle book, an encyclopedia, or on the Web.

Set up the maze experience before the youth arrive. Station leaders or post signs at some of the major junctions. There the youth should be faced with an ethical choice. One answer to the decision would mean they would travel down one path. Another answer would send them down another path. The right choice—the one that God would lead them in or that Scripture supports—is the way that will take them closer to their goal. Try to make some of the ethical choices more difficult than others.

On the way:

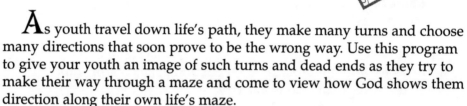

Have a little fun with getting to your destination this time. When you get in the vehicle, ask someone to tell you the first direction to go. Don't give any answers or hints, just begin traveling in the direction that is first suggested. When you come to an intersection, ask another person which way you should go. The first answer is the way you should travel. Try this for about ten minutes or periodically along the way to your destination. After a few minutes ask the youth if any of them have ever been lost. What did they do? Were they frightened? How did they get lost?

At the site:

1. Explain to the youth that as they wander through the maze, they will encounter some moral dilemmas. Tell the youth that when they encounter a leader or a sign that asks the question, "What would you do if …?" they should answer it. Their answer will determine which way they will turn. Explain that if they answer correctly they will find themselves nearer the goal of the maze; an incorrect answer could eventually lead them to a dead end.

2. When the youth have finished the maze, have them meet in one place and sit in a circle so that all can be heard in the discussion.

3. Ask:
- Were there any decisions that you had more trouble with than others? Which ones? Why?

Explain that the purpose of the exercise was to help the youth understand that God gives guidance in life, and we are most faithful when we discern God's will in our choices instead of doing only what we want to do.

4. Read Psalm 23.

Ask:
- How do you feel led by God in the paths of righteousness and beside the still waters (a place of safety and refreshment)?
- What instructions from God are the clearest for you?
- Which ones are the most difficult to understand or hear?

5. Read Matthew 7:13-14.

Ask:
- Why is the easier way the wrong way?
- Is the easier way sometimes the more enjoyable way, too? Why or why not?
- Why is God's way through a narrow gate?
- What does this Scripture and the maze have to do with your own life?
- Who has God set up in your life to give you good directions along the way?

6. Offer yourself as a guide for your youth to call on for instruction and advice in their own maze of life. Explain that there are others who are great at encouraging people to enter through the narrow gate. Ask the youth who they would put on such a list.

7. Ask:
• Why do we seek to follow the right path?

8. Make it clear to the youth at this point that we do not, and cannot, follow that path because we want to get to heaven. Explain that following Christ doesn't work that way. Making the right choices and decisions—living the right way—will not "earn" us a place or a "route" into heaven. That can only be done with faith in Jesus Christ and allowing him to be the guide through the maze. We seek to follow the right path, God's path, because we want to be obedient as an act of worship.

9. As a closing, take your group into the maze once again and walk to a dead end. Have the youth face the dead end and explain that a relationship with Christ will turn any dead end into a new beginning. Jesus has gone ahead of us and meets us at all the dead ends in our lives, giving us directions to continue and discover that the most joy-filled journey through the maze is the one that follows him.

DESTINATION Neighborhood —

Focus: Youth will link actual neighbors with Jesus' instructions to love our neighbors as we love ourselves.

Scripture: Luke 10:25-37; Leviticus 19:11-18

Location: The neighborhoods of several youth

When youth think of their neighbors, they think of people they know and live near. So why not travel to their neighbors and have the youth tell you a bit about them?

Youth will know some neighbors well, while others are virtually unknown. Each relationship the individual youth have with their neighbors is unique. Be careful not to make this program into a gossip tour. Remind the youth to speak with affirmation of their neighbors and to simply give insight into the people who live near them.

On the way:

Before driving, read Luke 10:25-29. This introduction will set up your discussion for the car. While you head to your destination, talk about one or two of your neighbors. Tell a kind story or account of what one of your neighbors has done. Try to keep the first destination a secret, if possible. Simply arrive at the home of one of the people in your vehicle. Everyone should remain in the car or van.

At each site:

1. When you arrive at each house of one of the youth in your vehicle, ask him or her to tell about the neighbors, pointing to each house. Youth might tell a story, naming all who live there as well as their jobs and ages and what kinds of things the neighbors enjoy doing. Then travel on to another house and do the same. Continue this way for a few people in the van (or everyone).

Bright Idea! This program could be linked with "Destination Road" (page 108), allowing a more concentrated look at the Good Samaritan story.

Notes

2. Next, travel to a part of town where no one in the van lives. Stop the van in front of a house and ask:
- Will someone tell me about their neighbors here?

Allow silence or comments of "none of us lives here" and move on. If there is time, drive to another location where none of the group lives and do the same, asking them to tell about their neighbors there.

3. Finally, travel to a location where much of the town can be viewed: a high hill overlooking the community or an area just outside of town where you can stop and look at the town. Stop there and get out of the vehicle.

4. Finish telling the story from Luke 10, starting over at verse 25 and going all the way to verse 37.

Ask:
- Who is your neighbor?

5. Talk for a few minutes about how the youth are or are not neighborly to the people they do not know.

Ask:
- What is a neighborly act?
- Is it easier to do a kind, neighborly act for someone who lives next door or for a stranger? Why?
- Tell about a time when you recently did something neighborly for someone you knew, for someone you did not know, for an enemy. How did you feel each of those times?

6. Read the laws from Leviticus. Explain to the youth that the Old Testament speaks very clearly on how we should treat others. Jesus took this group of laws that speak about how we treat our neighbors and gave faces and directions on who our neighbors are. A Samaritan and a Jew lived in neighboring countries, but neither was thought to act "neighborly" toward the other. In fact, Jews were told to shun Samaritans. They were thought to be "unclean." Yet Jesus made a point to use these two neighbors in telling us to love our neighbors as we love ourselves.

7. Ask the youth to think about someone (or a group of people) to whom they find difficult being "neighborly." Allow some time. There may be a section of town that they simply stay away from, a school district that is a rival and avoided, or a family that is shunned because of some rumor going around.

Ask:
- What would it be like if you were to start today loving that person or group of people as you love yourself?
- What might you do?

8. Have the youth think of an action plan of how to show an act of love for a few of those "shunned neighbors."

9. Close with a prayer, asking God for strength and help as you share the love of the gospel. Ask the youth to commit their action plans to God by saying, "Lord, I'm going to love my neighbor as myself by _____." Amen!

Notes

_____

_____

_____

_____

_____

_____

_____

_____

_____

_____

_____

_____

_____

_____

_____

DESTINATION

Focus: Youth will relate to Mary, the mother of Jesus, at the time of Jesus' birth and recognize that, just as Mary was called on to bear Jesus to the world, they are also called by God to bear Jesus to the world.

Scripture: Luke 1:26-38, 46-56

Location: A local hospital nursery

X YOU ARE HERE

A visit to a maternity ward nursery with newborn babies is a great surrounding for connecting youth to their own creation, their own birth, and the birth of Christ. Talk to some of the nurses at the maternity ward before bringing the youth. Tell them what you will be talking about and ask if they would be willing to help. If possible, you could ask a new mother if she'd be willing to talk to the youth when they visit.

On the way:

Begin in the hospital at either a waiting area that is not occupied or a table in the cafeteria. Spend some time finding out what the youth know about their own birth. What would they have been named if they had been the opposite sex? How old were their mothers when they were born?

MPH

Explain that Mary, Jesus' mother, was probably about fourteen or fifteen when Jesus was born. Yet God saw that she was worthy of bringing the Savior into the world. Tell the youth that you are going to be viewing some newborn babies. Encourage them to be very respectful and quiet during the walk through the hospital.

At the site:

1. Take the youth to the floor where the maternity ward is located and look for the nursery. If you've arranged for a nurse to speak with your group, have the nurse tell the youth about the tasks maternity and nursery nurses do. Allow the youth to ask a few questions and thank the nurse for speaking with them.

2. Read verses 26-38.

3. Ask:
- Why do you suppose God chose Mary to be Jesus' mother?
- What characteristics do you suppose Mary had to have in order to bear God to the world?
- What characteristics do you need to have in order to show Jesus to others?

4. If you've arranged to speak with a new mother, invite the youth to talk to her about how she prepared for the coming of this baby and what she expects in the days and months ahead. Once again, have the youth thank her for speaking with them. (It would be nice to have flowers or balloons for her.)

5. Move to an area where you will not disturb anyone and ask:
- How are you prepared this Christmas for God to enter into your life and world?
- How would you respond if you heard that Jesus was born today? to a teenage girl you know?
- How would you respond if God told you that you would bear God's son to the world today?

6. Explain that God has indeed told the youth that they are to bear Jesus to the world—by letting the entire world know about his birth, ministry, and resurrection. Ask them how they can become "God bearers" in their own schools, families, and community.

7. Tell the youth to listen to the words of Mary and place themselves in the role of one who is called to bear Christ to the world. Then read verses 46 through 55.

8. As a closing, read verses 46 through 55 aloud together. Then pray that your group would be open and willing to bear Christ to the world in everything you do.

Notes

DESTINATION  Pit

 **Focus:** Youth will examine psalms that speak of God's never-ending love and care as they journey into and out of a pit.

Scripture: Psalm 23; 40:1-3; 139:1-12

Location: A pit or canyon

In Scripture, to say that someone is in a pit means that he or she is in a state of misery and despair. If your youth have not yet felt such misery and despair in their lives they will, no doubt, at some point. They need to understand that God is even there in the lowest pit, loving them and offering them comfort and strength. Help your youth through all their lowest times by taking them into a pit.

The deeper the pit, the better. You'll want youth to experience the feeling of being in the bottom of a pit at times in their lives—past or future—when they feel low. There may be a number of possibilities for pits in your community, but one easy one is to find a construction pit of some kind. Get in touch with the contractor or land owner before taking your group into any pits. If you have canyons nearby, those would work just as well.

On the way:

Talk about moods and how the youth in your vehicle respond to a person in a bad mood. Do they try to solve other people's problems? Do they listen? How do they act when they are in a low mood? How bad does it need to get before asking someone else for help?

At the site:

1. When you arrive at the site, tell the youth to sit or stand in a group in the bottom of the pit. You may need to help them into the pit.

2. Ask the youth to sit (or stand, if the floor of the pit is too dirty) around the edge of the pit, facing the wall. Have someone read Psalm 23.

Ask:
- What is "the valley of the shadow of death" (NRSV)?
- Have you ever felt like you were in that valley?
- Have you felt God's "rod and staff" (NRSV) comforting you in that valley? If so, how?
- What comforts you most when you are in a pit of despair?

3. Ask someone to read Psalm 139:1-12.

Ask:
- At times, are you so down on yourself that you even want to hide from God?
- Where has the psalmist talked about "hiding" from God?
- What do you do when you feel despair or misery?

4. Explain that a relationship with Christ can nurture us and comfort us even when we are in the pit of despair. Jesus ministered to the sick, the grieving, the lost, the lonely, and the outcast. He himself was in anguish and was an outcast when he suffered on the cross. He understands and knows our pain and our loneliness, and he loves us in the midst of such pits.

5. Tell the youth that Jesus will bring us out of the pits we get into. Explain that God places people in our lives to help us out of the pit. By drawing on the strength and compassion of others and letting them know what you need, you have company and compassion. You need not despair in your pit. To show this point, have the youth help each other climb out of the pit. Call them by name as you lift each one.

6. When all are out of the pit, have the group stand around the pit's edge. Read verses 1-3 of Psalm 40.

Ask:
- What has God done for the psalmist?
- What does it take for you to be drawn out of your pits?
- Does God use anyone most often to help draw you out? Who?
- Do you know anyone who is in a pit now who needs someone's help?

7. Instruct the group to join hands beside or around the pit while you begin a closing prayer. Pray for the trust it takes to ask for help and the courage it takes to latch onto the hand of God as God lifts you out of the pit. After you have prayed, invite youth to continue praying either silently or out loud as their hand is gently squeezed. When an individual finishes praying, he or she should squeeze the next hand, passing the prayer around the circle.

Notes

Destination Power Plant

Focus: Youth will associate their visit to a power plant with God's power and how God uses that power through the Holy Spirit to work in their lives.

Scripture: Acts 1:6-8; 9:1-20; Matthew 17:14-20

Location: A power plant

The power of God's grace is truly amazing. In a day when people assume the quest for power is related to money, more weapons, greater political influence, or more resources, your youth need to be confronted with the truth of the gospel and the power of that good news. Introduce your youth to the power of God through this program at a power plant, and help them recognize that they can, indeed, move mountains.

Any type of power facility will do for this destination—a hydroelectric plant, a power station, or perhaps even high voltage wires in which your group can hear the "hum" of electricity as it flows overhead. If you are able to visit an actual station where power is diverted and distributed, call ahead to see if you can set up a tour of some kind. Any information you and your group can get will help the image of power in the gospel.

On the way:

Play a game of "Electric Shock" as you travel to your destination. Have each person hold hands (*not the driver*) forming a chain through the group. A "volt" of electricity is started by

squeezing the hand of a person in the chain. When an individual feels a squeeze, he or she should pass that on to the next person. There should be only one "volt" moving at a time. The driver of the vehicle calls "power check" any time he or she wishes. When that is called, the person still holding the "volt" gets a point, while the person who passed it on to him or her loses a point. The object of the game is to have as few points as possible including negative numbers. The driver can also call for a direction change by calling out "power switch."

At the site:

1. Talk to the youth about power.

Ask:
- What kinds of power are there in the world?

Youth may begin talking about "energy" power, which is fine. Ask if there are any other kinds of power. Move the discussion towards the "influence" type of power: politics, money, military, resources, name, and so forth.

2. Tell the group that you will be looking at power today and the kind of power that is the strongest of all—God's power.

3. If someone can take you on a tour of the power facility, begin the tour here. Allow some time for the group to ask questions. If you are not taking a tour, go on to step number 4.

4. Read the Scripture from Acts 1:6-8.

Ask:
- In what ways have you witnessed God's power?

Allow some time for the youth to think and talk about this. God's power is seen in the way God's Word influences everyone in the world—not just believers. God's power is seen throughout creation and through the laws of creation that God set up that are still at work in the world. God's power is seen and experienced when we experience God's grace and God's love. It changes lives, and in so doing, it changes all power structures of the world.

5. Ask:
- To what kind of power do you think Jesus was referring in the Scripture from Acts?

6. Set the context for the Scripture from Acts 9:1-20. Tell the group that the next Scripture they will be hearing is from Paul's conversion.

Say:
Saul, later known as Paul, was a devout Jewish leader who had permission from the Temple to seek to destroy the Christian movement. He was a persecutor of the Christians, seeking to arrest them and even aiding their deaths. Then, on his way to another city to find more Christians, this is what happened...

7. Read Acts 9:1-20.

Notes

_____

_____

_____

_____

_____

_____

_____

_____

_____

_____

_____

_____

_____

8. Ask:
- How did God's power influence Saul?
- How did it influence the world?

9. Read the Scripture from Matthew.

10. Ask:
- Have you ever felt that God had given you the power to move mountains?
- What kind of mountain do you think Jesus was talking about moving here?
- What mountains have you had to face that you needed faith in God in order to make something happen?

11. Explain that God wants the youth to use God's power but only if such power reflects God's glory and not their own. God's power is stronger and lasts longer than any power plant. Faith in God's power will allow youth to make mountains move.

12. Close in prayer, asking for the power to do God's work in the world.

DESTINATION

Public Square

Focus: Youth will experience God's grace.

Scripture: Ephesians 2:8-9

Location: A mall, city park, parking lot, or any busy place where there are lots of people

While this program will cost a bit of money (five dollars per small group), it's a small price to pay for youth to experience the power of God's grace and recognize how people sometimes react to such a free gift.

On the way:

Before you leave, break the group into smaller groups of about four youth and one adult. Give each group an envelope with five one dollar bills and several slips of paper (see below). Also give each group a copy of the four rules:

1. You must give each dollar bill away to a different person. The person cannot be a part of our youth group. You can only pick from this list, and each "type" of individual can only be picked once: a child, an older person alone, a woman with children, a person you know, a teenager with friends, a teenager alone, a couple (man and woman), an adult alone, and a family. This is not a race!

2. You cannot tell the recipients why you are giving it to them. You may only tell them that it is a free gift with no strings attached. You can tell them your name, but you may not tell them that you are with your youth group or with a church group. You also may not lie. If a person accepts the money, also give him or her a slip of the paper in the envelope.

3. If someone refuses the money, give him or her a slip of paper from the envelope and move on to another person.

4. When your group has handed out all five dollars, return to the church.

103

Notes

The slips of paper in the envelope should say the following:

We are from the youth group at First Church and are participating in a program that helps us look at how people respond to God's free gift of salvation. Some accept it wholeheartedly, some believe there must be strings attached, some are embarrassed, and some refuse the gift because of mistrust or pride. Your response to the "free money" may be similar to how some people respond to God's salvation. While a dollar is in no way equal to God's gift of grace, your response and our own struggle to "give away" this money will foster some discussion on this topic. Thank you for helping us in today's lesson, and may you also experience the power and blessing of God's grace.

Our youth group is studying this verse from the Bible: For by grace you have been saved through faith, and this is not your own doing; it is the gift of God—not the result of works, so that no one may boast (Ephesians 2:8-9, NRSV).

Spend some time talking about what the youth are about to do. Make sure they understand that they should not be burdensome on the people they encounter. Invite questions from the youth.

At the site:

1. Before the groups go out, read Ephesians 2:8-9 aloud.

Ask:
- Why has God decided to just give us this gift of salvation and not make us earn it?
- What does Paul mean when he writes, "so that no one may boast" (NRSV)?

2. When the youth finish giving away all their money, have them meet at a specified location.

Ask:
- What are ways that people respond to God's free gift of salvation?
- What ways did the people you met today respond to your free gift?
- Why do you think they acted the way they did?
- How would you act if a stranger came up to you and offered you something very expensive?
- What would help you accept an expensive gift from someone else?
- What stands in the way of people accepting God's gift?
- How can you help?

Notes

3. Point out to the youth that just as it is difficult to sometimes accept something from a stranger, so also it would be difficult for some people to accept salvation from a God they do not know. That is why God came to earth as Jesus—to allow us to have a closer, stronger relationship with God. We are called to help others build on their relationship with God by introducing them to the gospel and to Jesus Christ and by showing them the love of Christ.

4. Make a plan to follow through with one or more of the answers to the last question in number two ("How can you help?").

5. Close with prayer, asking God to touch the lives of each person encountered during this experience.

DESTINATION  Refiner's Fire

Focus: Youth will see that Jesus purifies us from all sin, making us sanctified, strong, and pure in the eyes of God.

Scripture: Malachi 3:2-3

Location: A kiln or refinery

A true refinery may be hard to find. Check the art, chemistry, or biology department at a local high school or college for a kiln. You could also look for an artist's studio nearby and ask if a kiln is available.

A refiner's fire is used to "cook away" the impurities in certain minerals such as silver, copper, and gold. The heat melts the mineral, liquefying it, and putting it through particular chemical changes, making it purer than it had been before. When clay is heated, the fire not only purifies the clay, but it also strengthens it into pottery.

Bright Idea! This program could work well in conjunction with "Destination Clay" (page 35).

You will need a handful of dirt, two pieces of pottery (one baked and one unbaked), and a container that is safe to put in the kiln. A day or two before the program, place half of the dirt in the container and cook it in the kiln for at least twenty-four hours. When it is taken out there should be only the minerals and stone. All the organic material has been destroyed by the heat. Save the other half of the dirt for comparison during the program.

On the way:

Ask the youth about a time in their lives when they got into big trouble for something they did.
Be careful not to glamorize any wrongdoing. Acknowledge what is shared and ask the youth how they tried to patch things up after their wrongful deed.

At the site:

1. Begin by helping the youth understand the purpose and the workings of a refiner's fire. The artist or refiner should show how the fire/kiln works. If a refiner or artist is not available, then you could use the information here and whatever else you might find to inform the youth yourself.

2. Read the Scripture.

3. Ask:
- Why do you think the writer of our Scripture passage uses the image of the refiner's fire when talking about our relationship with God?

4. Show the two samples of dirt—the one that has been cooked and the one that has not. Tell the youth that both samples came from the same place but one has been cooked in the heat.

Ask:
- Which do you think has been in the heat? Why?

5. Next, pass around the two samples of pottery: the "baked" and the "unbaked."

Ask:
- Which do you think has been in the heat? Why?

6. Explain that when a refinery burns away impurities in metal or when a kiln bakes the clay into pottery, then it makes those things pure and the clay stronger. In the same way, Jesus Christ takes away all of our impurities and our sin, and strengthens us; he makes us pure. This process is called sanctification.

7. Read the Scripture again, this time replace the words "the descendants of Levi" and "them" (verse 3) with "you" so that it reads "and he will purify you and refine you like gold and silver until you present offerings to the Lord in righteousness" (NRSV).

8. Explain that Christ has already done what is needed for each of them to be purified or sanctified. The real question is whether we accept Christ and his sanctifying grace. Ask the youth if they have made such a decision to be purified by God's refining fire.

9. Take time to allow youth to examine what it would mean to allow God to refine them. Give them an opportunity to pray silently and talk to God about what in them needs to be purified and made stronger.

10. When they are ready, close in prayer, asking God for the strength and courage to be made pure of our sins.

Notes

107

DESTINATION 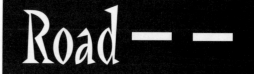 Road - - -

Focus: Youth will experience the parable of the good Samaritan first-hand and be equipped to lead a servant-minded and merciful life.

Scripture: Luke 10:25-37

Location: A rural road

Bright Idea!
This program could be linked with "Destination Neighborhood" (page 93).

The road symbolizes a journey we take, encountering Christ in many ways along the way. Jesus' story of the Good Samaritan is an example of three different responses to someone in need. Youth sometimes need help in recognizing who around them is in need and how God can use them to respond with love and compassion. The road can help youth focus on some of the needs around them, how they sometimes choose to respond, and how Christ calls them to respond.

You will need to set up this destination by choosing a road that is long with few interruptions—perhaps a stretch of road where there are no gas stations or houses close by. Safety would also call for this to be someplace other than an interstate. Find four adult volunteers posing as strangers who are willing to give a few minutes to serve as "victims" along the road. Assign the volunteers to one of three locations along the stretch of road, allowing at least three miles between each location. Each location should be set up to look as if they are in need. Some possibilities are a car with its hood up and flashers on, a stranger (or strangers) needing a ride, a car off the road in a ditch, or a person walking along the side of the road carrying a gas can.

On the way:

Explain to the youth that you have to arrive at your destination within twenty minutes or you will be too late to enjoy the experience. Act like you're in a big hurry. As you travel to your destination, make sure the route you take will pass by the three volunteers on the side of the road.

As you pass by the first stranger, go slow enough so that the youth can see what the problem is and that someone there is in need. Don't stop, but point out that you are in a hurry and are sure that someone will be along soon to help.

When you pass by the second stranger don't even say anything. See how many youth notice him or her and continue on your way. (It might even add that extra touch if the stranger were to try to flag you down or wave as if wanting you to stop.)

Finally, when you see the third stranger, make a point to notice him or her and ask the youth if they think you should stop to help. Don't let on that this is the actual person you were coming to help. If someone asks, point out that this person looks like he or she could use some help, too. After you get some responses as to whether you should stop or not, pull over (or turn back around) and stop to offer help.

At the site:

1. When you stop, ask the stranger if he or she needs help. The stranger should answer by stating what he or she needs. Ask the youth to get out of the vehicle in order to all help. (It would be best if this last volunteer is not one who simply needs a ride.) When everyone is out, start doing what is needed to help, trying to get everyone involved, if possible.

2. When you have finished helping (to whatever extent that takes your group) have the stranger suddenly start reading aloud the Scripture. Many youth will be caught off guard, but as the parable begins they may start getting a clue of what is happening.

3. Explain that this stranger you just served was actually a volunteer as you introduce him or her to your group.

4. Ask and discuss:
- Why did the priest and the Pharisee in Jesus' story not stop for the person in need?
- Who noticed the other two people in need on the way here?
- Did you think we should stop? Why or why not?
- Why did the Samaritan decide to stop and help the man on the side of the road?
- What did he risk in doing so?

5. Explain that this lesson is not teaching them to stop every time they see someone along the road. Emphasize that safety concerns are a factor. We may not be able to help everyone we see along the road. We can, however, be intentional about living a servant-minded and merciful life.

6. Have the group examine their own abilities to recognize those in need. Ask them to think of someone they have seen in the past week who needs something—anything—that they can give. Then ask the youth to pair off and tell their partner who they thought of and how that person could be helped. Be very aware of safety issues as they pair off. Keep them on the side of the cars that are away from the road.

109

7. After a few minutes bring the pairs back together and ask:
- What response does Jesus expect of us when we see someone in need?
- In verse 37, Jesus says to be like the Samaritan who showed mercy. How will we show mercy when we see a need?
- What are some ways we can help those in need during the course of everyday life?

8. As a closing, have the youth spend a moment in silent prayer asking for the courage to be merciful. Close the prayer by praying the Lord's Prayer.

DESTINATION

Rooftop ─ ─ ─

Focus: Youth will analyze how intentional they are in bringing their own friends to Jesus and be empowered to bring their friends to Jesus.

Scripture: Mark 2:1-5

Location: A rooftop

X
YOU ARE HERE

W hen Jesus was healing people in Capernaum, so many people gathered around that one could not approach the house where he was staying. In order to bring their friend to Jesus, a group of men actually tore off the roof of the house. How upset would the trustees of your church be if your youth were so "on fire" about bringing their friends to Jesus that they would tear a hole in the roof of the sanctuary if need be? Yet that's the type of fire we want from those who follow Christ. Take the youth up to a safe rooftop and help them assess just how "on fire" they are about bringing their friends to meet Jesus.

Try to find a rooftop where your whole group can stand or sit together for the duration of the program. Make sure you have a safe way of getting the group on and off the roof. A flat roof will be the safest way to use this program.

On the way:

Ask the youth to think about a time when they or someone they know wanted something so badly that they took drastic measures in order to get it.

At the site:

1. Before going up to the roof, ask the youth to break into smaller groups of no fewer than five. Tell each group to choose one person from their group who will be carried by the rest. Mark off a distance of about forty yards and explain that the groups are to move as fast as they can, carrying their teammate. The one to be carried is to lie flat and not help in any way (no holding of shoulders or sitting up).

111

Notes

Announce the start, and encourage each group as they carry their teammate to the finish line. If you have enough people for only one group, allow different people to be carried so they get the experience of carrying and being carried.

2. Move to the rooftop. Have the youth sit on the roof, if possible, in a circle facing in.

3. Talk about the race. Ask the youth:
- How far would you be willing to carry a friend?
- What would have made carrying your teammate easier?

4. Read the Scripture.

5. Ask:
- Why do you think the men didn't just join the rest of the crowd near the house?
- What made them think that it was OK to climb up on the roof and tear a hole in it?
- Would you go through such difficulty in bringing a friend of yours to Jesus? Why or why not?
- How far would you go to help a friend meet Jesus?

6. Encourage the youth to think of their friends or people they know who do not have a relationship with Jesus. Spend some time brainstorming about ways the whole group can help each other bring these acquaintances to meet Jesus. Suggestions could be planning a special event to hear a Christian speaker or performer or organizing a retreat that focuses on meeting Jesus and inviting those who need such an introduction.

7. As a closing, join hands and leave a gap in the circle. Explain that the gap is for those who do not yet know Jesus and who need to be brought to him. Ask the youth to name persons they think need to be introduced to Jesus. Then close with a prayer, asking God to help your group have the courage and motivation to bring these others to meet Jesus.

DESTINATION  Ruins

Focus: Youth will understand what a state of ruins looks like and compare it to their spiritual state.

Scripture: Ezekiel 36:33-36

Location: An area of ruins

Upon returning from exile, the Jews found Jerusalem in ruins. The prophets likened the ruinous state to that of their own walk with God. God assured them, though, that the ruins would be changed into a thriving land so that all who passed by would see that God was with them and was glorified.

Your youth have encountered or will encounter times when their lives seem like these ruins. Their faith walk has, at times, found devastation and ruin. Help them see the hope in a God who promises to help them rebuild their ruinous faith so that God will be glorified in all they do.

Any ruined building will do, but a home that is in ruins might be something the youth can relate to a little better. A home is a place where people live, and the image can be transferred to the way we live as well. You will need a new nail for each youth to help remind them of the repairs God is making in their own spiritual home.

Bright Idea! This program would work well around the new year as your group considers the state of their own spirituality and what parts of their faith need rebuilding.

On the way:

Ask the youth to consider all the different areas of their life—physical, school, family, friends, emotions, work, serving, future, spiritual, and any others they can think of. Ask them to tell a month of the year that would best describe how they are doing in that area of life. (For example, "I feel like July right now because everything is sunny in my life.")

At the site:

1. Go through the ruined house or area. Talk about each room as you enter. Discuss what the room was used for and what it probably looked like when it was in good shape.

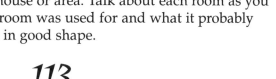

Notes

2. Ask:
- Have you ever found your life in the condition of this house?
- What kinds of things ruin houses or other physical things?
- What causes us to be in a spiritual state of ruin?

3. Explain that you will be reading a Scripture from Ezekiel that speaks of the ruins of the city and how they are much like the ruins of the people. God's people had been making bad decisions in disobeying God. God allowed them to be taken into captivity and the city to be ruined. This symbolized the ruinous state of their own lives as they let their relationship with God crumble. But the Scripture states that God will allow the people to rebuild the ruins and will bless them again so that the world will see them and know that God is at work in their lives.

4. Read the Scripture.

5. Ask:
- How can the condition of a house or a building be used as an example of the state of one's spiritual life?
- Using the house you are in (or were in) now, how would you describe your own spiritual life?
- What "repairs" can be made to make it even better?

6. Assure the youth that God will work in them to rebuild their own spiritual lives.

Ask:
- When your faith is strong and your spiritual life is healthy, who is the builder of such a "house"?
- When we try to build our spiritual house by ourselves, what is the result?
- How can you allow God to repair your own spiritual house today? this week? this month? this year?

7. As a closing, hand each youth a shiny, straight, new nail. Tell them that the nail will remind them that God will repair and restore them to their original beauty. Pray to be made new.

DESTINATION

Focus: Youth will better understand that Jesus Christ guards us from sin so we will not be devoured by it.

Scripture: Romans 6:11-14; Hebrews 9:23-28

Location: A scarecrow

The scarecrow is placed in a field in order to scare away some of the animals and birds that eat the crops. Jesus often used the field and the harvest as images of God's work in the world and the ministries of the faithful. If the crows are any of those things (sin) that would devour God's harvest, then the scarecrow is a wonderful image of a Christ figure who is set in the field of the world in order to stop sin from harming the harvest ever again.

If you cannot find a scarecrow in your community or local backyard, then you could easily make one. Another possibility is to have the materials at your fellowship hall and ask the youth to make a scarecrow. Try to find or make one whose arms are spread out like Jesus on the cross.

On the way:

Tell the following story of the scarecrow:
There once was a farmer who planted a field with crops. While watching his field one day, the farmer noticed birds swooping down, tearing out plants, eating seeds, and devouring some of the crop. The farmer said, "I will place in the field a scarecrow, and because of his presence in the field the birds will be afraid and will not devour my crops." So the farmer built his scarecrow and placed it in the center of the field where all the birds could see that the crop was not to be disturbed.

At the site:

1. Have the youth gather in a circle around the scarecrow. Read Hebrews 9:23-28.

Ask:
* How can sin devour you?
* What types of things help you not to sin?

2. Explain that Jesus does not stop sin from happening; rather, his presence and sacrifice in the world has made it so that those sins no longer separate us from God. As the scarecrow chases away the birds, so also Christ's presence in our lives stops our sins from devouring us.

3. Read Romans 6:11-14.

Ask:
* How can sin become our master?
* How can you stop that from happening?

4. Help the youth understand that we are all called to stop our sinning and that the only way we can do that is with the strength of God's Holy Spirit. If we could save ourselves from sin, then we would boast of not needing God.

Ask:
* How do we gain access to the power that "scares" away all sin?
* Do you trust Jesus to deal with your sin, or do you try really hard to stop sinning on your own?
* Will you trust Jesus to take your sin, or will you cling to it and let it devour you?

5. Pray for God's strength to give up our sins. Sometimes it's more comfortable to hang on to sin rather than be free from it. Praise God for devouring sin before sin can devour you.

DESTINATION

Shade Tree — — —

Focus: Youth will learn to understand God's mercy through Jonah's experience under a shade tree.

Scripture: Jonah 4:1-11

Location: A shade tree

The story of Jonah is a great teaching tool. Jonah was to go to a city and tell all its inhabitants that they are doomed by God. Jonah didn't want the job. Eventually, even after Jonah had completed his assignment, he became angry with God because God showed mercy to the repentant Ninevites. Jonah did not think God should have shown mercy.

Jonah went to the outskirts of the city because he was mad at God. God provided Jonah with shade there to cool him and to teach him a lesson. When God took the shade away, Jonah complained. But God wanted to teach him that just as Jonah cared about a shade tree he didn't make, God cares so much more for God's people in Ninevah.

Try to find the biggest tree that provides the most shade. Maybe your youth have a favorite park, or someone has a big tree in his or her backyard. This program works best on a warm or hot day.

On the way:

Ask the youth to talk a bit about times when they have been really angry. What did they do? What made them angry? Did they ever get over it? What do they often do when they are angry? Have they ever been angry at God? for what?

At the site:

1. Explain that you are going to spend some time under a shade tree and learn about another man who got angry at God.

2. Before reading the Scripture, set up the story by explaining what has happened up to chapter four. You could have the youth tell it if they know the story. Some of them will know some parts, so let them add what they do know and you fill in the rest.

117

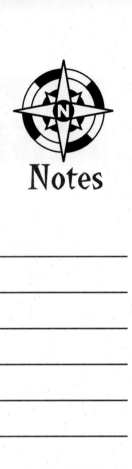

3. Read the Scripture.

   Ask:
   • How easily do you get angry?
   • What kinds of things make you angry?
   • Whom do you know who is slow to anger?
   • Why did Jonah get angry in the Scripture?

4. Explain that Jesus taught us to love our enemies (Matthew 5:44). Loving our enemies is hard to do when we also want to see them punished for the things they do that are against us.

   Ask:
   • What enemies do you have that you need to learn to love?

5. Talk for a few minutes about mercy—namely, God's mercy. To understand God's mercy, one must realize it is given to the undeserving.

   Ask:
   • How can showing mercy be powerful?
   • Which is more likely to change the hearts of someone doing wrong: strict punishment or mercy and compassion?

6. Jonah was basically throwing a temper-tantrum in this passage. He thought God should act in a different way than God did.

   Ask:
   • Have you ever been angry with God for not doing what you thought God should do?
   • Why were you angry?
   • Do you believe that God knows what is best for you?
   • Is it easy or hard to trust God?

7. Point out to the youth that God, in fact, does know what is best for us. God loves us through the times we are angry with God. Thankfully, God shows mercy because God is mercy. Mercy exhibits God's love.

8. Take a moment to feel the shade of the tree. Have the youth lie down around the tree and soak in the shade. Tell the youth to think of the shade they feel as God's mercy that covers and cools them. Have them remain lying around the tree as you close in prayer praising God for being merciful. Ask God to remind them of God's mercy when they experience anger.

DESTINATION

Sheepfold

Focus: Youth will examine whom they follow through life and learn to follow the Good Shepherd.

Scripture: Isaiah 40:10-11; John 10:1-18

Location: A sheepfold at a farm or petting zoo

It is understandable that sheep are referred to so often in both the Old and New Testaments. Shepherding has been a way of life for many in and around Israel for thousands of years. Scripture writers have made use of the image of sheep and shepherding because it is one that God's people understood. The image of the shepherd can be helpful for us today. When you help your youth understand this image, you open up the intent of the Scriptures to them, allowing God to use the Word in strengthening their faith.

A sheepfold, in biblical times, was a walled enclosure built either of stone or of a thorny hedge. It had a narrow entrance through which only one or two sheep could walk at a time. The sheepfold was a place of refuge and protection for the flock in times of danger. A number of flocks would be kept in a single sheepfold at a time. At the gate was a watchman. When the shepherd from a certain flock came to the gate for his sheep, the watchman would open the gate and the shepherd would call his flock. Only the sheep that recognized his voice would follow their shepherd out of the gate, leaving the other flocks behind.

When you set up your destination, ask the owner of the sheep if he or she could spend some time speaking to your group about sheep. Any information that can be given about shepherding and about the instincts of sheep will help your youth understand the Scriptures a little better. If you do not live near a sheep farmer, you could use this program in a petting zoo.

On the way:

Ask the youth to think about those whom they follow. How do they decide whom to follow in certain actions or decisions—in the way they dress, the movies they see, the people with whom they socialize, or the people with whom they

Bright Idea! If you plan this destination in the spring, you may be fortunate enough to see lambs. If your timing is right, there may even be a birth while you are there!

do not socialize. What stars or famous people have they decided to follow in certain areas? Why? How much do they follow the media? pop culture? the Bible?

At the site:

1. Introduce your youth to the owner of the sheep and allow the youth about five minutes to touch and become familiar with the sheep. If you are holding this meeting in a petting zoo, allow the youth some time to pet and feed the sheep.

2. Have the youth gather where they can hear you. Explain to them that the Bible has many images of sheep and shepherds. Ask if anyone can give some examples of those images. After a few examples are given, ask:

- Why do you suppose that image is found so often in the Scriptures?

3. Invite your speaker to tell a little about shepherding and about sheep in general, allowing some time for questions if there are any. If you do not have a speaker, find out any information you can about shepherding and tell it to the youth. Talk about what it means to be a shepherd.

4. Read Isaiah 40:10-11.

Ask:
- About whom do you suppose the writer of this Scripture is telling?

Explain that Isaiah was a prophet and that this Scripture, written years before Jesus was born, is prophesying that God will send the Messiah. This Scripture is a description of the Messiah. Read the passage again.

5. Tell your group you want them to gain an understanding of sheep and what it means to belong to the flock of the Good Shepherd so that they can relate those characteristics to Jesus Christ. Then tell the group that Jesus talked about himself as a good shepherd in the Gospel of John.

6. Read John 10:1-18.

7. Ask:

- In what ways are we like sheep?
- How is Jesus like a good shepherd?
- Why do sheep follow the voice of the one with whom they are most familiar?
- With whom are you most familiar? Is that whom you follow most?
- How can you become more familiar with Jesus?

8. Point out the characteristics in the Scripture that have helped the sheep learn to trust their shepherd and how those characteristics fit Jesus. Some of these are:

- The shepherd enters the sheepfold by the gate—by the appointed way. (Christ entered into the world in the ways prophesied. He was born of a virgin—Isaiah 7:14; Matthew 1:22-23. He was born in Bethlehem—Micah 5:2; Luke 2:4-7. He was born of David's line—2 Samuel 7:16-17; Matthew 1:1-17.)
- The shepherd's own sheep recognize his voice and follow him. (Those who already follow Jesus know his words and teachings.)
- The shepherd lays down his life for his sheep. (Jesus laid down his life for each of us and would never sacrifice us in order to save himself.)
- The shepherd seeks those who are lost. (Everyone is important to Christ. No one can stray so far from God's love, that Jesus does not continue to seek the lost one.)

9. For a closing, ask the youth to think about ways they can grow so close to Jesus Christ that they automatically follow his familiar voice. Close with a prayer, asking God to help everyone there become more familiar with Christ than with anyone else.

Notes

DESTINATION  Soup Kitchen

Focus: Youth will gain an experience of serving those in need while relating such an experience to their preparation for the coming Messiah.

Scripture: Luke 3:4b-14

Location: A soup kitchen or meal shelter

In learning to serve others we prepare ourselves for the coming of Christ into the world again. Jesus said that he was returning and that we should be ready. In the Scripture passage, John tells us that we are to share coats and food with those who have none as we prepare for Christ's coming. A trip to the local soup kitchen will allow the youth to experience service and learn about preparing the way for the Lord.

On the way:

Tell your youth that you are going to take them all to lunch. On the way, ask them what they do to prepare for an upcoming event. Name a few events that would involve preparation: a date, worship services, a prom, graduation, Christmas, hosting a party, an operation, a family movie night, and so forth.

At the site:

1. Explain to the youth what they will be doing. Have the leader of the kitchen give details of where help is needed and assign tasks for the youth. As the youth prepare for the meal, move around the group and affirm them. Help them understand that they are serving Christ today.

2. When the guests arrive, help the youth serve as needed. If possible, have some of the youth spend time talking with the guests.

3. Don't forget that you promised to treat the youth to lunch. When the meal is over and the clean-up duties are completed, gather everyone at a table and enjoy a meal together. Once everyone has begun eating, read the Scripture.

4. Ask:
- What do you do to prepare for the coming of Christ?
- Do you spend as much time preparing for his coming as you do for Christmas or a party? Why or why not?
- According to John the Baptist, how can you prepare for the Messiah's coming?

5. Explain that preparation for Jesus' coming is a good reason why we serve others as you did today.

Ask:
- What did you learn in your experience today with the guests?
- How did this experience help you prepare for Christ's coming?
- How did it remind you of Christ?

6. Have the group examine their level of commitment to serving Christ. Talk about their experience and ask if they would be willing to set up a regular schedule of service in their community. Discuss possibilities and an action plan for consistent service.

7. Close with a prayer, asking God to help each of you prepare your hearts for the coming of Jesus Christ so that your lives will show it in your actions. Pray also for those whom you served and will serve in the months ahead.

Notes

DESTINATION  Starry Night

Focus: Youth will connect God's promise to Abraham with a sky full of stars and with their own lives as being a part of the fulfillment of that promise.

Scripture: Genesis 15:1-6

Location: A starry night

Have you ever stood in awe at a dark sky covered with bright, shining stars? The best view is on a cool night away from any city lights or highways. As you and your youth travel to this destination and spend some time staring up at the starry night, you will set in their minds a memory and a link with God's Word for them.

Choose a place where the stars are exceptionally bright and where there is a clear view. Since the youth should lie down on their backs while looking up at the stars, you may want to take blankets. As an added teaching aid, try studying a star chart ahead of time so that you can point out a few constellations to your youth. Or perhaps you know someone you can invite to teach about the stars.

You will need a copy of "Sometimes by Step" by Rich Mullins. It is from *The World As Best As I Can Remember It, Volume 2,* or *Songs.* You will also need a battery-operated boom box.

Bright Idea!

If you are coming home late at night from some type of outing or trip and are ahead of schedule, try pulling off into a park or field and going through this program.

On the way:

Play a game of "I Spy." One person says, "I spy something red" (or shiny, or whatever color, shape, or texture something is that the person can see). The others try to guess what it is that the person "spies." A guess is made by asking, "Is it the license plate on that car?" or whatever is seen that matches the description that the first person gave. When a person guesses the object, that person gets to "spy" the next object. As you near the destination, say, "I spy something bright" and let them guess "the stars" to conclude your game.

At the site:

1. Ask the youth to lie down and look up at the stars. If the group is not too big, ask the youth to lie with their heads together so that people can be heard easier and so that everyone is looking pretty much from the same place. Spend some time pointing to different stars and constellations. See if anyone can spot a shooting star or a satellite as it makes its way across the heavens.

2. Tell the youth that long ago God spoke to Abraham about these very stars and had a particular star in mind that represented each of them. Then read the Scripture.

3. Explain to the youth that God chose Abraham to be the father of a great nation of people. Because God chose Abraham, the world would be blessed (Genesis 12:3). God directed Abraham's attention to the stars in order to give him an image of just how many descendants he would have. One of those stars, then, can represent each person in your group.

4. Suggest that each person pick out a star that would represent himself or herself. Tell the youth to figure out a way to find that star easily in the years ahead. Talk about why they chose their star. Remind them that God has always loved them and has always had a plan to bless each of them since the time of creation. When God spoke to Abraham, God used the stars to remind Abraham that each time he looked upon a starry night he would see the number of his descendants. God also wants your youth to remember that, though they are a few of millions, each is an individual and set in place here by God for a purpose. Invite the youth to remember their own uniqueness and God's blessing for them each time they look upon a starry night—and especially when they seek out their own star.

5. Play the Rich Mullins song, "Sometimes by Step." It is from *The World As Best As I Can Remember It, Volume 2*, or *Songs*. Encourage youth to sing along, paying special attention to the lyrics. You may want to read the verses and ask the youth to join together in singing the chorus. Another option is to find the sheet music before your trip and arrange for a guitarist to play the song while the group sings along.

6. Ask the group to keep their eyes open and gaze upon the stars as you close in a prayer. Pray for God's grace and blessings to continue in the lives of your youth. Pray that your group would fully understand how unique and beautiful they are in God's sight.

Notes

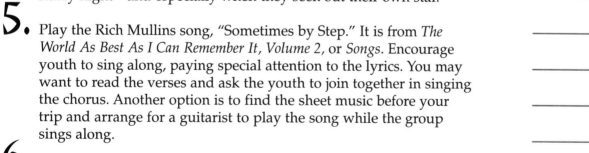

DESTINATION

Focus: Youth will link a tower or long stairwell with our own struggle to "earn" our way into God's kingdom.

Scripture: Exodus 20; Mark 10:24-27

Location: A tower or long, multi-story stairwell

The community that built the doomed Tower of Babel thought that if they could build a tower to the heavens, then they would become like gods. Too often we humans view our good works and compliance with God's Law as something that will get us closer to heaven. No matter how many times we hear the good news of God's grace, we fall into the trap of thinking that what we "do" earns our way into God's kingdom. Youth will learn that it is impossible to earn such merit, and that Jesus Christ is the only means by which they can achieve their goal. This program is most effective if there is an area on the top floor where youth can look out at the world around them.

Be sure to choose a destination that is safe and receive permission from the building's owner. Church or school bell towers, city clock towers, high rise buildings, or a fire watchtower are some examples of towers. You will need ten stops along the climb where youth will respond to a question. You will also need one adult for each level (nine adults in addition to yourself).

Bright Idea!
If you are fortunate enough to have a skyscraper with an observation deck in your city, try taking the stairs instead of the elevator and have the discussion when you get to the observation deck.

On the way:

Talk about reasons people believe they should do good works. Some answers may include the following: to please God; to get into heaven; because God tells us to; because we want to imitate Christ. Don't affirm any certain answer. Acknowledge them all as reasons people have for doing good. What are examples of good works?

At the site:

1. Explain to the youth that their goal is to reach the top of the tower or stairwell. Point out that the climb up will represent our attempts to please God by "doing" something. Explain that they will be allowed to ascend to the next level when they recite each of the Ten Commandments. Each team will have one piece of paper and a pen to write down their answers. The adult at each level will initial it and give back to the team to present to the adult at the next level. Divide the group into smaller teams of no more than four or five people in each team.

2. Spread the start times over a few minutes so there will be space between teams. Begin by taking the first team to the starting point and away from the other teams. Ask the youth in that team to tell you one of the Ten Commandments. When they answer correctly, allow the team to climb to the next level. Youth will continue this process until they reach the last level. Have an adult volunteer at each stop to receive the answers and initial the teams' papers.

After one team has ascended to the second level, the next team should begin their ascent. As teams get closer to the top, some may fail to remember the last few commandments. If they do forget, they must remain on their current level. They may ask for help from other teams that pass by, but they may only ascend to the next level when they correctly name a commandment that they have not already named.

3. If any youth reach the top by reciting all Ten Commandments, congratulate them. Would they have reached the top if the requirement for ascending were to have never broken a commandment?

4. Some groups may not be successful in reaching the highest level. For those, an adult leader should make his or her way back down the steps, stopping at each stalled group. Read Mark 10:24-27 to the group, emphasizing verse 27. Then ask the stranded youth to claim another reason, according to that Scripture, that should allow them to reach the top. Youth should recite verse 27 (especially "for God all things are possible" [NRSV]).

5. When everyone has reached the top of the tower read from Mark 10:24-27 again.

6. Ask:
   • Why do you think Jesus said it is impossible for someone to be saved?
   • How do you think the disciples felt when they first heard that?
   • How do you think they felt when Jesus said, "for God all things are possible" (NRSV)?

7. Ask:
- What if you had to "earn" your way to heaven by obeying all of God's commandments?
- How far would you get? Would you keep trying?
- Why is it so hard for us to accept that we don't have to "do" anything to gain God's favor?
- What does it take to be saved, if for humans it is impossible?
- Why do you suppose God decided to give us grace?

8. Jesus said it is impossible for mortals to be saved. In other words, we cannot save ourselves. Thankfully, nothing is impossible for God. God sent Jesus to be our way. We need not place our trust in our ability to "do." Our efforts will not get us any closer to God. Christ brings us as close as possible. Let us do good works, not to earn God's favor, but as an act of worship.

9. From the top of the tower, ask the group to look out over the surrounding area. Tell the youth to pray silently for God to continually remind them of the power of God's grace. Then, after a minute of silent prayers, close by reading Mark 10:27b: "For God all things are possible" (NRSV).

DESTINATION Tree ─ ─ ─ ─

Focus: Youth will experience the perspective from which Zacchaeus saw Jesus and examine their own perspective.

Scripture: Luke 19:1-10

Location: A tree large enough for climbing

W hen Zacchaeus saw that Jesus was coming towards him and that a crowd of people were in the way, he looked for something that would allow him to view the Savior. For Zacchaeus, the best way to see Jesus was to climb a tree. From the lofty spot in the tree, he could look on as Jesus passed through Jericho.

Be sure to choose a tree that is big but safe enough for everyone to climb or gather around the trunk. In order to create a setting like the Scripture passage, find a tree that is in a busy park or where there are a lot of people.

Before the day of your meeting, ask an adult to portray Jesus as the story is told. Ask a few others to act as a small "crowd" of people who will congregate around the trees and then run to meet "Jesus" when he starts walking towards the group.

On the way:

Tell about a time when you were or weren't  picked first for a team. Tell the youth what that felt like for you. Then ask the youth if any of them have ever been picked first for a team and what it felt like.

At the site:

1. Before you begin the discussion, allow the youth to climb the tree. Those who do not wish to climb should stand around the trunk and look on. Explain to the youth that you want them to climb the tree so that they can gain a different perspective on the story they are about to hear. Allow about fifteen minutes for climbing.

Bright Idea! This program would work well on a high ropes course (especially one with large trees). Wait until your whole group is up high in the course and begin the discussion.

Notes

2. Ask:
- What can you see from up in the tree that you could not see from the ground?
- Why is having a different perspective on things often important in any situation?

3. Read the Scripture or tell the story in your own words. As the story is told, have the person playing Jesus and the small crowd you have assembled begin playing their roles. Jesus should begin walking towards your group. Have someone from the small crowd recognize "Jesus" and exclaim, "There he is!" The crowd should then run to meet the man. As you continue telling the story, Jesus should walk closer to the tree, stop, and look up, choosing one person from your group to point to as you narrate Jesus' calling to Zacchaeus. At this point, tell your actors to sit with the group.

4. Ask:
- What do you think Zacchaeus felt like when Jesus pointed to him and chose to stay with him?
- What feelings did the people of the crowd have when Jesus picked Zacchaeus? Why?

5. Explain to the youth that everyone in Jericho was trying to see Jesus. Out of all the people gathered, Jesus chose Zacchaeus. Zacchaeus was not popular. In fact, he was disliked very much. He had been a cheater and a thief in his career as a tax collector. But Jesus said he came to seek out and save the lost. Zacchaeus changed his sight perspective so he could see Jesus, and in turn, Jesus changed his life perspective.

6. Ask:
- What might be stopping you from seeing Jesus in your life?
- How could you change your perspective in order to see him more clearly?

7. Gather around the tree and hold hands. Pray for Jesus to give you a better perspective to see him in your life.

DESTINATION

Wall – – – – –

Focus: Youth will experience the importance and the blessing of tearing down walls that divide different people and cultures.

Scripture: Ephesians 2:12-16

Location: A wall

Climbing a twelve-foot high wall is an obstacle that can be a fun experience of teamwork. But for this program, the wall represents something much more harmful to the group's spirit. Paul uses the image of a wall as a barrier or division between two groups of people. Because Christ has broken down every wall, we can be free from the boundaries that separate. Christ has made us one. This program will help your youth experience that unifying spirit of God.

Many camps and recreation centers have a special wall that has been constructed for a program such as this. The best wall is about twelve feet high and ten feet wide with a platform on the top back side for those who have climbed to stand and help the next climber.

Instruct the youth that this exercise demands complete trust. Joking, pushing, demeaning of others, or begrudging is not allowed. Everyone should be encouraging of one another.

Some youth may not want to climb the wall. Encourage them to try, but do not pressure them. Those who do not climb should remain on the ground to cheer on the climbers.

On the way:

Talk with the youth about things that cause hostility between groups of people. Ask what walls divide groups of people in their own schools. What actions keep those walls up? What actions tear them down?

At the site:

1. Explain that the goal of this activity is to get the whole group over the wall by working together. Those who are not climbing must help by offering aid, spotting other climbers, and giving encouragement.

Warn the youth that if anyone says anything negative to another person, then the whole group must return to the ground and start over.

2. Without announcing it, quietly note that the youth who have made it to the top can go back to the front side in order to help people over the wall. Wait and see if someone suggests or offers it as a strategy.

3. Begin the activity. Adults should oversee and encourage the youth.

4. When the youth have successfully climbed the wall, gather them to begin the discussion.

5. Ask:
- How hard was it to climb the wall?
- Was it easier or harder to work together?
- Is it harder to work with others or to work independently to get something done?

6. Read the Scripture.

Ask:
- Where do you have a dividing wall of hostility in your life right now?
- What helped you get over this climbing wall today?
- How is this exercise similar to what Jesus can do with our walls of hostility and division? How is it different?

7. Explain that the wall these youth climbed over was not torn down, as Christ does to our walls. When we allow a wall of hostility to stand and we just "work around" the problem, then we are allowing that wall to become a permanent area of bitterness in our lives. This Scripture passage assures us that Christ has broken down the walls that divide.

8. Ask:
- How do we hinder Jesus from breaking down those walls?
- Do you feel like you stay divided by walls, that you climb over those walls, that you work around the walls, or that you allow Jesus to break them down?

9. Ask the youth to dream about what their life would be like right now with no hostility or division—no family tensions, no cliques at school, and no racial or international tension. See if anyone would like to describe his or her dream.

10. Explain that Jesus doesn't just help us get over walls. He tears them down, destroying those things that divide us or cause strife.

Ask:
- How does a relationship with Christ put hostility to death (verse 16)?
- What can you do that would allow Jesus to tear down those walls even further?

11. As a closing, join hands and ask the youth to visualize a wall that is keeping them from someone or something. As they pray silently, tell them to imagine Jesus' tearing down the wall brick by brick, until it is demolished. After a few minutes, pray for courage to face hostile situations with an attitude of confident peace because of Jesus Christ.

Notes

DESTINATION

Well ---

Focus: Youth will turn to the Living Water and be inspired to share it with others.

Scripture: John 4:1-26; Psalm 42:1-2

Location: A well

Thirst is an image that your youth understand. All creatures relate to being thirsty. Perhaps Jesus used thirsting and hungering as teaching tools because he knew the image would stand the test of time. Sure enough, even today we can fully understand what it means to be thirsty, drink some water, and an hour later become thirsty again. Help youth hear this Scripture lesson in a new way by taking them to a water well. Youth will make the connection that our physical bodies will always thirst for water, but our souls need never thirst again because Jesus is the Living Water.

If you do not have access to an actual water well, you could visit a local "watering hole" where your youth often like to hang out or a drinking fountain at a park or in a shopping area. The benefit of these options is that the youth will see a drinking fountain or hangout again, while a well is not the center of a day's activities as it was in Jesus' day.

Bright Idea! This program could be done at the end of a long, hot hike where the group stops for a drink. As they drink, talk about how nice it would be to be able to drink and never thirst again, then move into the program as you fill up your water bottles.

On the way:

Ask the group to tell about a time when they were very thirsty. What quenched their thirst? Ask them to tell about a time when they were the hungriest they'd ever been? How long have they gone without food?

At the site:

1. Gather around the well and allow the youth to send a bucket down for water. Bring along cups for them to drink the water. If you are gathered around a drinking fountain, allow everyone to get a drink and then be seated for the discussion.

After a few minutes ask:
- What if you found a source of water that could quench your thirst forever?
- Would you drink the water?
- Would you bring others to drink? Why or why not?

Notes

2. Explain that Jesus talks about such a water source in today's Scripture. Tell the youth that today's Scripture passage has a lesson within a lesson. Set the context of the Scripture. Explain that Jesus had been traveling back to his homeland, Galilee, which meant that he had to travel through Samaria, a land where the people were of mixed race—Gentile and Jew. Because of the intermarriages, many devout Jews of Jesus' day considered it wrong to even enter Samaria. They were clear that a Jew should not talk with Samaritans, especially not the women.

3. Read the Scripture.

4. Ask:
- In your school, is there a group of people with whom it is not acceptable to hang around? Who?

5. Explain that Jesus' offering this woman living water is most significant because she was a Samaritan woman. Jesus rendered this woman worthy of the life-giving water, a woman who was looked down upon because she was a Samaritan and because she was a woman. She was also looked down upon because she was living with a man who was not her husband. She came to the well at noon (the sixth hour)—the only time of day when prostitutes were allowed to draw water. By society's standards she was not worthy to receive such a blessing. Jesus, however, changed the rules and proclaimed that all who would seek the Living Water shall find it and quench their thirst.

6. Look again at the Scripture. Reread verse 14. Then read Psalm 42:1-2.

Ask:
- What kind of water are Jesus and the psalmist talking about here?
- What kind of thirst?
- Have you ever experienced a thirst for God in some way?
- What is thirsting for God like?

7. Remind the youth that Jesus was offering the woman at the well this life-giving water.

Notes

_____

_____

_____

_____

_____

_____

_____

_____

_____

_____

_____

_____

Ask:
- What must one do in order to receive such water?
- How does that relieve a thirsty soul?

8. Explain that God created the soul as the means for a relationship with God. So it is understandable that, when we live our lives apart from God, our souls get "thirsty." Tell the youth to imagine walking for miles without stopping for water. Days go by and still no water. The throat becomes dry. The tongue swells and sticks to the sides of the mouth. Eventually the body cannot exist and begins to die. Likewise, the soul longs for what can quench its thirst. A personal relationship with God through Jesus Christ is the only way to quench the thirsty soul.

9. Talk about ways to offer life-giving water to those who have not yet heard the message. Discuss ways to reach out to those whom society deems unworthy.

10. As a closing, ask the group to sit in a circle, shoulder to shoulder, facing inward. Pass out cups of water and ask each person to serve the person to his or her left in the circle, saying, "Receive Jesus Christ, the water that quenches your soul." Allow a few minutes of silence for youth to savor and think on this experience. End with a prayer asking to be continually filled with the Living Water and for the courage to share it with others.

DESTINATION

Wilderness — —

Focus: Youth will recognize that God is with us in the wilderness times, giving comfort and order.

Scripture: Psalm 107:1-7; Exodus 15:22-27

Location: A wilderness or desert area

The wilderness theme in Scripture indicates a place for wandering, of very little water, great danger, and filled with wild animals and roving bands of raiders. Today, we think of the term *wilderness* as a beautiful area where city lights do not interrupt the starlight and the noise of traffic cannot be heard. Because of this difference in the biblical and the modern view of wilderness, your youth may not understand some of the references to the wilderness in the Bible. Use this program to enlighten your youth, so that each time they are in their own "wilderness" they will appreciate God's presence there and the clarity with which they can hear God's voice.

If possible, find an area of wilderness that is somewhat bleak—a dry riverbed, an open prairie, or desert. Try to find the most desolate area within your driving range. Desolation will help the youth understand the connection between desolate land and desolate souls. Thick woods would be an appropriate location, but stay away from the most beautiful wooded areas.

Bright Idea! This program would work well as a follow-up to "Destination Bonfire" (page 26).

On the way:

Talk about how they would feel if they were alone for a month. How would they cope? What thoughts would enter their heads? How would they prepare for the experience? Move the discussion to times when they have felt forsaken, lost, or lonely.

At the site:

1. Tell the youth to walk around the area looking for signs of disorder, danger, and desolation. Give them about ten minutes. When they return, have them tell or show what they found.

Notes

_____

_____

_____

_____

_____

_____

_____

_____

_____

_____

_____

_____

_____

_____

2. Point out that in Old Testament times the wilderness consisted of any place beyond the boundaries of government or civilization. The wilderness was thought of as a dangerous place where one had little control of what might happen. Wild beasts, bands of savage wandering tribes, and even evil spirits were among the expected dangers in the wilderness. Today most people long for a chance to get away from the city and rest in the wilderness.

Ask:
- Why do you suppose people feel better about being in the wilderness today than they did thousands of years ago?
- If you were out here with no one else around, no car nearby, and no road or path in sight how would you feel?

3. Read Psalm 107:1-5.

Ask:
- What does the psalmist mean when he says, in verse five, "hungry and thirsty, their soul fainted within them" (NRSV)?
- What might cause you to feel like your soul is fainting within you?
- What are some times when you or those you know have felt lost as if you are in a wilderness with no direction and with danger lurking all around?

4. Before reading Psalm 107:6-7 and Exodus 15:22-27, ask the youth to listen for how God's presence in the wilderness helped bring comfort and security.

Ask:
- How did God bring hope and direction to those struggling in the wilderness?

5. Explain that it is often easier to hear God's voice when we get away from the busyness of life and step out of our comfort zones. In the same way, when we are in our own wildernesses—when we are lonely and in despair or danger—we may find ourselves ready to rely on God and listen to God's guidance. We can also find more clarity with which to hear God's voice when we separate ourselves from the things that hold our attention.

6. Invite the youth to "wander" (but not too far away from the group) into some part of the wilderness alone for about twenty to thirty minutes. Ask them to listen for God's presence with them. Tell them to spend some time in prayer, asking God to be a very real and recognizable strength in all their wilderness times.

7. Call the youth back together and ask if anyone would like to tell about his or her experience. Close with prayer, thanking God for being with us in all places of our lives.

Notes

_____

_____

_____

_____

_____

_____

_____

_____

_____

_____

_____

_____

_____

_____

_____

_____

DESTINATION Wrestling Mat

Focus: Youth will link time spent on a wrestling mat with Jacob's own bout with God and remember the benefits of working through their faith struggles with their Creator.

Scripture: Genesis 32:22-32

Location: A wrestling mat

W hen Jacob wrestled with the angel of the Lord, his life was so changed that he received a new name as well as a limp in his walk. Your youth have no doubt wrestled over issues of faith and hopefully will continue to do so throughout their lives. These "wrestling matches" with God can be milestones in their faith development. Use this program and a visit to a wrestling mat to help the youth recognize the growth that can happen the next time they wrestle with God.

One of the best places you could find for this destination would be a gym at your local school. If the coaches there are willing to let your group use the mats, then the youth will be reminded of this time when they return to the gym on following school days. It would also be helpful to invite an adult who could talk about wrestling. While some of your youth may not feel comfortable rolling around on a mat with others, they may enjoy some tumbling or simple arm wrestling as others test their skills against each other.

Remember feelings and anxieties during this program. Do not let the youth get angry with those they wrestle. If it looks like unhealthy competition or anger is becoming a part of the experience, change the wrestlers and let someone else try. Remember that the point of this program is not to find out who is strongest or who can overcome another. The point is for the youth to connect a wrestling match with the way they struggle with their faith issues.

On the way:

Ask each youth to lay his or her hand out on a flat, hard surface (a window will work—it need not be horizontal). Tell them to lift each finger—one at a time. Next, ask the youth to curl all but the first finger under, against the hard surface, so that only that finger is straightened out. Once again, have them lift that finger. They should go through each finger. When they reach their ring finger, they will discover that they cannot lift it off the hard surface and still keep the rest of their hand on the surface. (Watch to be sure they don't "cheat" by raising the knuckles of their folded fingers.)

Encourage them to struggle with it for a moment, then talk about persistence. If they have an issue with which they are struggling, do they face it immediately, ignore it until a better time, or try to ignore it completely, hoping it will go away? How do they confront their struggles?

At the site:

1. Have the youth take off their shoes and do some stretching on the mat. Don't say anything about wrestling yet, just get everyone to sit and stretch on the mat.

2. Ask the youth to sit in a circle facing in. Set up the Scripture by introducing the character of Jacob to the group. Explain that Jacob, a name that means "grabber," cheated his older brother out of his birthright, taking his inheritance and blessing. Jacob feared for his life and so he escaped to a far away country and married two wives. Eventually he knew he had to return to his homeland and confront his brother. This Scripture begins on the night before Jacob was to meet his brother, Esau, for the first time since Jacob ran away. Jacob knew God's claim on his family and remembered God's call to him, so this night he was struggling to determine what he should do.

3. Read the Scripture.

4. Ask the youth to pair up and stand, facing each other on the mat. Their legs should be about shoulder width apart, and they should stand about two or three feet from each other. Tell the partners to place their palms on the palms of the partner about chest height. Next they are to try to push, without gripping with their fingers, their partner so that he or she moves his or her feet or goes to his or her knees. The partners should try this struggle three times.

5. Read the Scripture again.

6. Have the partners sit facing each other. Ask them to tell each other of a struggle they have had in the past few months—some sort of difficult decision they had been trying to make. Suggest they think of any struggles they have with persons or fears or something in the past.

Notes

_____

_____

_____

_____

_____

_____

_____

_____

_____

_____

_____

_____

_____

_____

_____

_____

Notes

_____

_____

_____

_____

_____

_____

_____

_____

_____

_____

_____

_____

_____

_____

_____

Ask:

- How can a personal struggle be like a wrestling match?
- How was Jacob's struggle like a wrestling match? With whom was he wrestling?
- Have you ever wrestled with God?
- What are some spiritual struggles that you are aware of in the Bible or in people you know?

7. Explain that Jacob's struggle with God that night led him into a closer relationship and better understanding of who he was in the eyes of God.

Ask:

- Can you think of any struggles in your life that made you stronger as an outcome?

Talk about some of these as youth are willing.

8. Ask:

- How can this group pray for you and encourage you in your spiritual struggles?

9. Close with a prayer for group members, asking for God's help as they wrestle with God's instructions and guidance.

SCRIPTURE Index————